Dancing with Dolores

James Holyfield MBE

ISBN13: 978-1-09943-176-0

Dedications

This book is dedicated to:

All the surgeons, doctors, oncologists, nurses, physiotherapists, radiologists, auxiliaries, porters and cleaners whose skills gave me extra time.

All my friends and family who gave me more help and support than I could have hoped for.

Lesley Cramp who encouraged me to write and helped me find the title for the book.

Special thanks goes to my partner John whose good humour and positivity pulled us through.

.

CONTENTS

Prologue

I have been a bit poorly of late.

I know this to be true because I now have a hole in my tummy where a feeding peg was fitted, bits of my spine are missing, I have two metal rods in my neck to stop my head falling off, carbon fibre to support my throat and a dent below my Adam's apple to show where a tracheotomy was fitted into my windpipe, plus some impressive scars at the front, side and back of my neck.

These physical changes were necessary to deal with a particularly nasty, rare and complicated bone cancer that was eating away at the spine in my neck. But having cancer does not have to be scary. Of course I wish I had not had it, but I did, and I dealt with it by turning everything that happened to me into a learning experience and I became fascinated with what was happening.

I am sure my partner, friends and family suffered more than me as they worried and I am convinced they think me mad or a least a little odd. But I had a duty to my marvellous surgeons who had the grisly job of cutting me open, skilled doctors who bombarded me with radiotherapy and the medical staff who nursed me back to health.

It was my job to count my blessings so I could be grateful for living in what is probably the best country in the world, work positively with the medical staff and show my nearest and dearest how strong and determined I could be, so they could feel better about my predicament and offer me the support I would need to live a bit longer.

Back in September 2016, I was told I would need two operations and a course of radiotherapy to deal with my rare cancer. It had been suggested that the run of the mill radiotherapy may not work and that I might have to travel abroad for proton beam radiotherapy after I had had the two massive operations.

I was assured the operations would rid me of most of the tumour but I would need to deal with the residual bits. I might have to go to Switzerland, Boston or Jacksonville in Florida. And all this would be paid for by the NHS.

Oh yes, I nearly forgot, along the way I also suffered a blood clot; my own little embolism.

1. Pain

'What a person did when they were in pain said a lot about them.'

Veronica Roth

I first felt unwell during the summer of 2015. During the second week of June, my partner John and I were coming to the end of our annual visit to Ireland when I got a mild pain in my neck, which over the next twelve months would get worse. I put the pain down to a muscle strain caused by painting the outside of John's family house where his sister Joan lives. John is from a village on the west coast of Ireland overlooking Ballyheigue Bay. The village stands on a beautiful three mile beach looking out towards America. The family house had always been a friendly fun place where John's mother had entertained her family and friends. Even though this wonderful and larger than life matriarch was now sadly gone, the house was still full of her personality. Like rich seams, her sense of fun was etched into its walls. She had never really left the home and it had remained an open and friendly place that people visited to have fun.

Three years earlier we had renovated the house by building an extension at the back. The house now boasted a large entertaining space in a new kitchen diner and a walk in pantry, downstairs shower room and a utility room.

Upstairs it has two new bedrooms and an ensuite bathroom, which was lovely except we now had a lot of new walls that needed painting. We agreed the whole house needed to be painted and not just the new extension. The front of the house and all the garden walls would also be given a facelift. We started at the front. A Polish labourer known to Joan was hired to help and John's brother Brendan was roped in because of his expertise at painting and decorating. Brendan proved to be the star of the show when he climbed up to places others would not dare.

The morning to start painting arrived and the weather was glorious. Normally I get up and make tea for John, Joan and me, but on this particular Tuesday Joan woke us with tea, biscuits and lots of enthusiasm. She wanted us up and out working. However, out of the six days we spent painting the house this was the only day we saw Joan before nine thirty. The events of the first day tired her physically and the amount of work destroyed her enthusiasm for the task. But Joan was happy to make drinks and buy items from shops that we needed to finish the job.

We agreed to start on the front of the house because it was one flat surface and the wall was not as high as the back because the back has a huge gabled roof. The front would be where I would do my apprenticeship. We got the paint ready. The brute of a ladder was put against the front wall. Armed with my paint and paint brush I climbed the ladder. I had never been up a ladder before. I was totally unprepared and I had never really thought what it would be like. I made the climb rather gingerly and when only halfway up I panicked. I froze, wobbled a bit and squeezed my eyes shut. I climbed down even more slowly than I had climbed up. I stood on the grass looking up at the bedroom windows taking in deep breaths. Why did the house not look so high off the ground when looking out of the bedroom window on lovely sunny days? I thanked God I was on my own standing in the garden. I told myself off.

'This is stupid. You're being daft. Take a few deep breaths and get back up there you prat. Think about what you will see. You'll have a lovely view of the beach. The sun is shining. Come on, we can do this.' I decided 'we' was me and my strong bits that do not let me fail at things.

I walked back to my nemesis and told this foe I refused to be scared of something made from aluminium.

'Are you okay James?' our neighbour Mary asked me.

Mary was talking to me over the garden wall. Unbeknown to me she had been deadheading her roses. I do not think she heard what I had said, but she had caught me having an argument with a ladder.

'Just planning what to do next Mary. We're painting the house Mary. You know, giving it a facelift,' I babbled.

'Shut up James,' I said to myself. 'You're beginning to prattle on and you already look weird.

'Well you've picked a good day for it. Let's hope it stays dry. It'll rain tomorrow, mark my words it'll rain tomorrow. Oh and welcome home. Say hello to John for me,' and with this our kindly neighbour went back in doors.

I dropped my head, sighed and looked into the bucket of paint, took a deep breath, squared my shoulders and tackled the ladder again. It was easy peasy and up I went full of my new found confidence. I was above our bedroom window painting the wall. I was right about the view; it was different from just looking out of the window and it was beautiful. The sun was shining on the wide expanse of pale sand and its rays were blurring the wriggly lines of the calm waves. I could hear the comforting sound of kids enjoying the thrill which only the sea can bring and I just caught the faint fresh smell of ozone.

'Wow you've started already,' John shouted up to me. 'How's it going?'

'Easy peasy, no problem,' I lied, but I did tell him later what really had happened. He loved the fact Mary had been watching and listening to me over the wall.

Climbing up and down ladders and stretching to reach difficult bits of the house was exhausting. On top of this we worked longer hours than a paid painter would because the property was ours. So at the end of the visit I thought a sharp pain I felt in my neck was down to all the hard work.

One of the last jobs was to paint the concrete caps on top of the garden wall we shared with Mary. I had been so careful not to let our colour go over to Mary's side. The line was near perfect. Because I thought it looked so good, I went indoors to see what it looked like from the front window. As I admired my work, a sudden pain that stabbed me in the neck was so hard I had to sit down. It would be more than twelve months before I would meet my guardian angel and find out exactly what was going on.

After our return to London the pain was there all the time. I visited my doctor who only prescribed some pain killers. Even though the pain was mild at first it never stopped. It was there twenty four hours a day and over the next few months it just worse. Out of desperation I tried different things to ease the pain that summer.

At this time I was a regular visitor to a gym where my personal trainer showed me some exercises to help strengthen my neck muscles. This did ease it a bit but the pain would always return. I also had deep tissue massages at the gym and again the relief was brief. On a trip to Spain in September I had trouble lying flat on sun beds. The signs were not good.

It all seemed odd I was having pain after painting the house in Ireland and visiting Spain for a week's holiday. I was growing superstitious about how the letters p,a,i and n might be affecting my health and even decided to avoid any activities or visiting places that used this sequence of letters in their names.

By early autumn the pain was starting to cause me serious problems. I was on holiday again in Ireland during the second week of October, when we stayed in a lovely hotel in Kenmare with friends. One night at dinner I could not turn my head to talk to the friend sitting next to me. It was also getting difficult to reverse cars because my movement was becoming restricted. I would need to make an urgent visit to my doctor on my return to London.

The GP I saw at the practise asked me what I wanted done. I had no clue and sat confused. I thought it was her job to advise me; wrong. She suggested more pain killers or physiotherapy. If I had known better I would have insisted on an MRI scan, but at this stage my knowledge of the medical world was limited to measles, chicken pox, reflux and the odd cold. I had not even had the flu before. I had enjoyed good health. When I was a teenager my father's brother said I was disgustingly healthy.

The doctor thought I might have arthritis so I asked if physiotherapy might help. 'Private or NHS' she asked me. 'NHS' I decided. I did not want to spend money on something that might not work. The GP had not sounded that optimistic. It was something to try; an experiment. I left with the expectation that someone would contact me within the next four weeks. Someone contacted me after two weeks, but the appointment to see a physiotherapist would not be for another six weeks on 17th December. So I carried on taking the painkillers, which did not actually do anything but I hoped they might have a placebo effect. You live in hope when pain is your constant companion. I had been in pain for nearly five months and it was getting worse.

Then it happened, the pain exploded. I woke up on December 14th screaming. The pain was so bad I actually thought I had broken my neck. I could not move. But I could scream and swear. This did not really help but I had to do something. My neighbours must have heard me and goodness knows what they must have thought because the language was disgusting. John rang the National Health Help Line 111. The lady did not hesitate. She sent an ambulance and I was taken to the emergency department in St Mary's. The paramedics did not seem that concerned. Perhaps they are hardened by their experiences, or perhaps they thought I was bluffing; even mucking them about. No bones were sticking out. We were moved over to another part of the hospital where we sat with others waiting to see a doctor.

When I needed to scream and swear I went outside into a back alley. Some maintenance men who were working on complicated looking pipework did not react to me at all. They just ignored my screams and swearing which amazed me, but I did wonder what they told their wives or partners when they went home that evening.

'You'll never believe the nut case who turned up in casualty today. He wouldn't shut up. And the language, you should have heard the language. Poor bastard.'

The doctor called me in. After examining me he told me my posture was off centre. My left shoulder was higher than my right. Then he said he had the same thing, where he got pain because of an old sporting injury. In his case the cause had been playing rugby. I have never been into sports so I doubted if mine was down to overexertion. I had wanted to be an actor. Reading Shakespeare under a tree when I was younger was not going to cause me a serious injury. But he prescribed more painkillers and told me to buy a good pillow. We left. If he had only sent me for an ultrasound, X-ray, CT or MRI scan we might have discovered what was going on in my neck earlier.

It would be another seven months before I finally found out I had an extremely rare form of bone cancer. And this would be more than twelve months since I first felt the pain after admiring my handiwork.

Three days later I kept my appointment with the physiotherapist who I saw three times that winter.

Even though the pain had caused me to be rushed to casualty, I still made the most of all the Christmas and New Year celebrations.

We went to a fancy dress party, hosted a few dinner parties, went over to Ireland for a weekend party in a castle near Knock and enjoyed the Pantomime in Wimbledon. We made a visit to the Victoria and Albert Museum to see the new 1600 galleries. Our visits to the V&A are really an excuse to have lunch or tea somewhere.

One of our traditions is to have an annual Christmas party in a restaurant with a group of friends. This annual event goes back to my fiftieth birthday party, when I hosted a supper in a private wine cellar on Regent's Street. Following one of these suppers, a body was discovered in the broom cupboard on Boxing Day in the area next to where we had our drinks reception. The poor chap from an Eastern European country had been sleeping in the broom cupboard and working as a cleaner. I often wonder what would have happened if one of my friends had opened the cupboard mistaking it for the toilet.

Christmas day was brilliant; I even did a twerk standing on a chair which ended up on Facebook. Who would have guessed I was in pain?

We spent New Year in Seaford on the south coast with our friends Justin and Alan. We met Justin and Alan through our mutual friends Neil and Nichola. Neil and John have worked together for over twenty years. At the time Justin had not been keen to meet John and me because we are over twenty years older than him and to use his words he was always worried that if he liked us he might end up being 'old queened'. During the three days in Seaford the weather was atrocious. The wind and rain were fierce. I had forgotten to pack socks so Nichola and I went into Seaford to buy some. The shop assistant asked if we were having a good time. We said yes except for the weather.

'Oh yes,' she replied. 'We do suffer from wind down here.' Nichola and I left the shop giggling like a couple of naughty school kids.

In between visits to the physiotherapist John and I went to Cape Verde for a week to celebrate his birthday. John was born on March 17th, which for an Irishman is just great because this is, of course, St Patrick's Day. You could never forget to send him a card. One morning we went on a jeep safari. This was not the best or wisest thing to do. The drivers went over the roughest terrain they could find. I was thrown around in the back of the Land Rover for three hours. I held my neck and prayed for the trip to end. To top it off we never saw a thing we were promised. We drove to a beach to see Lemon Sharks. They were out. We went to the turquoise grotto to see the sea rushing into a blue hole in the cliffs. The sea was brown and calm. We drove across the middle of the Island to see a mirage. We were told we would see an oasis if we crouched down and turned our heads sideways. I had been thrown around so much I could hardly stand up straight and crouching on the ground was not going to happen. A few of the punters said they could see the oasis; but I was not convinced. We went to the salt mines to float in the lakes. Actually that was brilliant. The salt flats are in the crater of a huge volcano that you have to walk into. The scene does take your breath away.

On our return from Cape Verde I made my third and final visit to see my physiotherapist who suggested I be referred to a skeletal department in a local hospital. I was still in pain. She did explain that getting a referral might be difficult because of budget cuts. However, she promised to present my case as strongly as she could. She also gave me a telephone number, which she told me to ring if I had not heard anything after six weeks.

During the first week in May we travelled to Scotland for a short holiday on a luxury train called the Royal Caledonian. It was a great excuse to dress up for meals and to drink some of the forty or more really excellent single malts. The passengers on the train came from Australia, the USA, New Zealand, Norway, Italy and Clapham. I used the trip to try and manage the pain by having lots of fun. One night we even danced on Dundee station wearing evening clothes. Exhausted commuters returning to Dundee did not appear to think this unusual or strange and went about their business. Or perhaps they were just tired and hated to see us being silly.

In the middle of May I rang that number and I asked the man from the booking centre if he had received my details from the physiotherapist. He said he had. I asked him when he was going to contact me. He said he was not, because of shrinking budgets. Shrinking budgets sounded so much nicer than budget cuts. I imagined a big canvas bag full of money simply deflating and getting smaller. It seemed hopeless and I felt sick. But he told me he was pleased I had contacted him. I asked for an appointment. He said this would be almost impossible. I pleaded with him by stressing I had been in pain for nearly a year. He took my number and said he would ring me back. I hung up and gave up. I thought I would not get a return call. I would have to go back to my GP and chain myself to the railings.

But in less than ten minutes he rang back and offered me not one but three appointments at different hospitals. He asked me which hospital I would like to visit. I accepted the appointment at Chelsea and Westminster Hospital on the Fulham Road because it was the earliest; not because it was the most convenient. Sadly it was not for another six weeks, but this would be okay because we were going to be in Ireland again for three of them.

Our trip to Ireland was wonderful. We went in the car and on the ferry to Rosslare. I was worried about driving that far because of the pain, but our car is comfortable and I used the headrest to support my neck.

We had been there about ten days when I went into the bathroom one morning to get ready. I was going to shave but was shocked at what I saw in the mirror. A swelling had appeared on the right side of my neck. It was more than a bump or a lump and the swelling covered the whole right side of my neck from under my ear down to my collar bone. It had come up overnight. I went back into the bedroom to show John. We could not do much at the time, but we knew I had an appointment at the hospital back in London so we tried to be philosophical about it.

Later we went to Kinsale to visit one of John's nephews whose wife Lisa Mc is an operating theatre nurse in Cork. I asked her about the swelling and she told me to get it checked as soon as I got back to London. I might have been wrong, but I thought Lisa Mc looked concerned. She was sure it was not caused by arthritis. The pain in the neck would often lay me low in Kinsale and I had to lie on the bed several times.

The weather was incredible and we had over two weeks of brilliant sunshine. We went for walks to the Black Rock. This walk is wonderful because you walk on the beach for three miles to reach a large rock that rises out of the sea. You do see other people walking but when the tide is out the beach is so wide you can only wave at them in the distance. I always go in the sea and then run along the beach to dry off. John and I usually climb up on the Black Rock where we sit in the sun and rest for a while before walking back to the village. The top of the rock is covered in thick grass which is lovely to lie on.

One of the beauties of this part of Ireland is that in the summer it does not get dark until after ten o'clock and you can sit outside enjoying the warm evenings. Even if the temperature drops you can light a fire and sit inside looking at the sunset through the window. When we are home we keep John's mother's traditions alive by having an open house. Loads of friends and family come to visit us when we are there. People come to play cards and talk. I normally bake scones or make a banana and walnut cake. Some days I might wash the cups a dozen times and we normally have a couple of dinner parties and family in for Sunday lunch.

Just before we were due to return to London, I began to feel much weaker and had to visit the doctor because I was suffering from diarrhoea. The doctor even gave me suppositories, which I had never used before. I thought this was totally embarrassing and threatened to kill John if he told anyone. It was bad enough I knew the lady in the chemist who dealt with my prescription. I imagined what she must know about the health of all the Ballyheigue residents. I was glad to be leaving the day after tomorrow. We left early in the morning to get to Rosslare in comfortable time.

We had booked ourselves into one of our favourite bed and breakfast establishments, a large country house, set in its own grounds. It has grand bedrooms and does a really wholesome freshly cooked to order full Irish breakfast. The lady who owns it told us that when she was a little girl growing up in the local village her father had been the chauffeur to the family who lived there. As a little girl she had promised herself that one day she would grow up and buy the house, which she had done. I was in awe of such an ambition fulfilled.

I was feeling lousy but we went out for dinner to the local spa hotel. When we arrived we had to run in to the hotel through a torrential downpour. That lovely summer was over.

On our return I had a bath. I stood up to dry myself and I saw myself in the mirror. I did not look unwell. My body was toned from visits to the gym and I had one of the best suntans ever. My white marks shone out from my hips. I convinced myself there could not be much wrong with me. It was an awkward moment but I did manage to put a suppository where it needed to go. To avoid this hateful moment, I had even contemplated swallowing it with some water. I could not get used to the procedure, even though they did seem to be working. I put on a pair of shorts and went to bed. John was watching the end of a programme on television and I fell asleep in the huge comfortable bed. I was able to make full use of the big duvet because of the unexpected drop in temperature.

The journey back to London was tough. But we got there. Relieved to be home again I could now look forward to meeting the skeletal technician.

2. Dancing

'Diseases are not cured by giving them a name.'

Marty Rubin

I met my first angel.

'What would you like from this consultation?' my guardian angel asked me.

'A proper diagnosis please if that's possible. I'd like to know if there is something wrong with me.'

I had already had a long conversation with Sandra, the skeletal technician, so she knew how long I had been feeling ill and in pain. Sandra had also felt the swelling on my neck and I was beginning to feel confident I was in good hands. I had met my guardian angel on the same day Mike Tyson met Evander Holyfield to induct him into the Boxing Hall of Fame and confirm they were goods friends. Evander told the audience he had forgiven Mike for biting off part of his ear twenty years earlier. I was not sure if I could forgive the doctors who had not sent me for tests and who had only given me painkillers.

'Okay, let's do it,' Sandra said as she pushed her chair back from her desk with determined authority. 'Let's see what we can do.

Give me a couple of minutes to make some phone calls. Would you mind waiting outside?'

I went back out to where John was waiting. I told him I thought Sandra was trying to organise some tests but I was not sure. We did not have to wait long. Sandra appeared and asked us to follow her.

'We can talk on the way and I can tell you what will happen.'

We went to one of the upper floors for an X-ray. I sat waiting and Sandra went off to work her magic. By the time I had had the X-ray Sandra had organised for me to have an Ultrasound the next day, a CT scan in one week from now and a MRI scan in two weeks. The receptionist printed off the dates for the scans. We had only just met Sandra, but John was already beginning to look more relaxed and relieved that someone was taking control and doing something constructive. We did not know it at the time, but meeting Sandra would save my life.

After my X-ray, Sandra walked with us back to the ground floor. We thanked her for all her help and stepped out into the noisy and congested Fulham Road. I would not see Sandra again but thanks to her efforts. I was now in the system and would be looked after by some of the most highly trained, qualified, skilled and experienced people in their fields of expertise.

Before meeting Sandra and since arriving back in London from Ireland, I had been getting worse and the pain was now starting to affect my ability to do things. On the Sunday before my meeting with Sandra we had lunch at my friend Pauline's house. The weather was good enough to have lunch in the garden. On the previous Thursday the country had voted to leave the European Union and because the media were telling us civil wars had broken out in families and between friends we wisely agreed not to discuss Brexit. I was not sure how my friends had voted and I was not sure how their politics might have changed since our college days where I had met Pauline, Howard and Meryl.

The four of us have been friends for forty five years, but there have been breaks when we had not seen each other because of family and career commitments. I had not seen Pauline when she was busy bringing up her two children. Every year we exchanged Christmas cards and I would always write on my card to Pauline 'Love to the Girls.' Then one year Pauline told me in her card that one of her kids was a boy. I had not read her cards closely and had read the name Daniel as Danielle.

The four of us had been drama students together; sharing flats in North London. One particular flat in Bounds Green had running water, which could be taken for granted back in 1973; but we had not expected it to be running down the walls. It was so cold we used to sit in the kitchen with our feet in the oven. One Saturday we were going to see an opera at the Colosseum on St Martin's Lane. We had spent all our money on a box, which Howard thought was truly decadent but we were so poor we could only make pancakes. To make matters worse, we did not have an egg between us and we ate a gluey grey mess sprinkled with sugar. We had trouble hearing the singers over the noise our stomachs made.

I remember meeting Meryl on the first day at registration in an area of the college known as Crush Hall. You had to sign up for particular classes. I had not read the prospectus and was clueless so I took my lead from Meryl. Later in the week Meryl introduced me to Pauline and a lifelong friendship was born.

I got to know Howard a bit later. We were doing an improvisation class about the creation and Howard was picked to play God. He was required to get under a huge heavy tarpaulin and on cue from the lecturer was told to wake up and wail so the world could be created. I was having trouble taking the class seriously. On cue he woke up. He started wailing and shouting and thrashing about. Howard was brilliant. He adlibbed and shouted about creating the earth and the fishes. The tutor started to panic.

'Okay darling. You can stop now. Super. Well done,' she wanted to involve the rest of us who were to be trees, fishes and other animals. Howard could not hear her under his massive tarpaulin and carried on creating the earth, heaven and stars. I got the giggles. The giggles became uncontrollable and I was sent out of the room at 18 years old. I had never been sent out of a classroom before. I could not believe the lecturer could not see how ridiculous the whole situation was. I stood in the hall laughing so much I got a coughing fit.

I made a vow to be more serious next week, but it was impossible because we had to pretend to be Alsatians and all I wanted to do was fight and be frisky. When the class finished I waited for Howard. I wanted him to know I was not laughing at him and we went for coffee where Howard laughed so much he cried. We have been great friends ever since he created the universe.

The four of us have stayed in touch. We started meeting as a group when we saw each other again at Meryl's wedding. We each hold a dinner party once a year and John and I usually take the Christmas slot. Since we started working less, the four of us also meet regularly for lunch somewhere in the West End.

I enjoyed college but I was never really sure why I was there. We studied drama and English and we were supposed to end up in the teaching profession. I was not sure if I wanted to be a teacher but I did like the acting bit.

The main reason I went to college was to break away from home in a kind way. I did not want to simply leave home, which would have upset my parents, especially my mother.

I had great parents who put up with the odd way I often looked at things. At school, my father had supported my right to grow my hair and wear a tie dyed vest. As he predicted, it would only last a few days into the autumn term of my upper sixth year.

I needed an excuse to leave home and college provided the excuse. I was eighteen and I had outgrown my hometown. I also knew I was different. I did not go out with girls like my friends from school. I liked girls and had great friends of the opposite sex, but I was more likely to lust after their boyfriends. I did not know at the time I was gay but I knew something was going on and I wanted to explore my feelings and have other experiences. Fortunately for me and the rest of the human race I did not have a particularly aggressive sex drive. I did not have had my first sexual experience with another man until I finished college.

The early 1970s were fun but they were not great. Society was still repressed and role models were either non-existent or shockingly poor and inaccurate. Television was airing programmes like 'Love Thy Neighbour' and 'Are You Being Served'; I liked the camp character Mr Humphries, but I did not want him as a role model. I wanted my role models to be more like the thoughtful Burt Lancaster or the handsome Paul Newman, but gay. Masculine actors from recent history whose films I watched on the television on a wet Sunday afternoon. And the comedians on the programme called 'The Comedians' were using gay people as the butt of their jokes. The first time I plucked up courage to walk into a gay bar was horrendous but above all lonely.

Every holiday I always wanted to leave college. I would go looking for jobs. I was offered a few as well, including one to train as an auctioneer in a Mayfair Gallery and another as a trainee manager of a West End restaurant.

I probably thought teaching was for me because I attended a brilliant school. At the time I naturally assumed all schools were the same and as good as mine. This is not true of course and my school experience was rare. The school ran on strict lines and there were rules, but within the rules we were allowed a lot of freedom and were encouraged to have our own views. We had a debating society. All teachers were encouraged to discuss their subjects with us to make them more interesting and relevant.

We were told not to accept what we were being taught at face value and to question what we heard or read in books. The head teacher had been a prisoner of war in Japan and when he opened the school in the early 1960s he refused to lock anything away. He wanted his pupils to have access to all the resources the school had to offer. We respected the materials and equipment. He handpicked teachers who bought into his philosophy of education. The school had a youth club and pupils could complete the Duke of Edinburgh's Award. The variety of clubs meant you could take part in all sorts of sports. There were art, drama, chess, music and photographic clubs.

On the first day of school the head teacher introduced the deputy head.

'You can leave this school with as many qualifications as you need. That is up to you. But I can promise you this, the boys will leave as gentlemen and the girls will leave as ladies.' With this that inspiring woman sat down and smoothed her skirt across her knees, her face set with a look of determination. A pin hitting the floor would have been the only noise in the large hall if one had been dropped. No one said a word. Her words had given everybody something to think about. I have always believed those simple but inspiring words must still be spinning somewhere in space.

So I left the school able to think about everything. As I met more and more people I discovered I viewed the world differently to most of them.

My way of looking at the world and responding to problems was going to help me face up to the diagnosis that was just around the corner.

I ended up teaching in a pretty rough school in a relatively poor area of North London. I quickly discovered I was not a great teacher. I could keep kids entertained, but I am not sure they learnt much and what they did learn would not have been much use to them.

My downfall was I took the kids problems home with me and I fretted about their predicaments. I developed a skin condition. My doctor at the time advised me to leave the school, not the profession. He was sure I was a good teacher but he said I needed to toughen up and learn more about the world. So I went off to do that, with the intention of returning to the classroom when I was about twenty eight. It seemed like a good plan, but it did not happen.

Life outside was different and exciting. But I did miss the class I looked after. They were tough, imaginative and a bit of a handful.

Other teachers moaned about my class but I protected them furiously and told other teachers to engage with their enthusiasm. I was convinced they behaved badly because they were annoyingly creative.

One day my annoying form class had been creative again.

'Mr Holyfield, a word please,' the head teacher called me into her office. A room I had not seen before. I thought it was over personalised and I did not like her choice of pink wallpaper, which was more suited to a boudoir.

'Do you know the pupils in your form class are gamblers?' she said the word gamblers with a loud quivering voice in the manner of a hammy Lady Bracknell. I did not say a word and waited for her to continue. 'They are running a betting syndicate. On a Friday they draw lots about what you might wear on Monday morning. They are gambling Mr Holyfield. Each betting slip describes one of your different outfits and colour combinations. The one that accurately describes what you are wearing on Monday morning wins the kitty. The best lot to draw is the one that says you are wearing something new.'

'I suppose that must be the joker,' was all I could think to say in reply. We sat looking at each other. Again I waited for her to speak.

'This is not funny Mr Holyfield. What are you going to do about it?' I did not hesitate.

'Nothing; I think this is fabulous. Imagine stopping such innovation. Let's think about it. They are working as a team. They collect and keep safe the stake money. They are organised. They work out the odds. More importantly, they are not falling out or fighting. I always knew my class was clever. They are budding entrepreneurs. Besides they will grow bored of it and it is bound to die a natural death in a couple of weeks.' I could see the strait-laced head did not agree. The only crime I could see being committed was my love of clothes and how much I enjoyed wearing them. I would need to keep this in check.

'Mr Holyfield I demand you stop this now,' she shouted and in her frustration she went the same colour as her inappropriate wallpaper. I refused and before the Easter holiday handed in my notice. I left at the end of the summer term loaded with presents from my little bunch of budding entrepreneurs.

Pauline brought out the lunch but I was in agony by now. I tried to be cheerful but the pain was really bad. Ever resourceful, Pauline produced a collar to put around my neck which she heated in the microwave. It smelt of warm oats and it did help a bit. Pauline told me to take it home if it helped. When we left the pain was horrible and I did not really want to drive the car back into central London. Everybody kissed me and wished me luck for my hospital appointment the next day and I agreed to let them all know how I got on.

After meeting Sandra and my first X-ray, I returned to the hospital the following day for the ultrasound. The technician looked worried. I asked him what he had seen, but he assured me they would know more in a couple of weeks. I was beginning to feel a bit apprehensive and looked for distractions to take my mind off what was happening.

The next weekend provided a welcome distraction when we went to a wedding in Essex. This group of friends knew I had been to the hospital and they wanted to know more than I could tell them. They could see I was in pain but I did not want to second guess what was happening to me or spoil the celebrations. Even though I thought something more serious might be going on I still danced like a lunatic and had a great time. Breakfast on the Sunday was hard work because the pain had got even worse but I put this down to the late night and the dancing.

It was a pity but John was not going to be in London when I was due to have the CT and MRI scans. John had to go to Bermuda for his job. The trip had been planned weeks before and because I was only at the testing stage I told him to go as planned. He left on Tuesday and even before his plane took off I was back in Fulham having my CT scan. As the engines on his plane were being revved my CT scanner was being charged. I had the MRI scan one week later. My GP rang me the day before and urged me not to miss the appointment. He said it was essential I have the scan. I did not think to ask him why or to enquire about what he had been told or to whom he had spoken. I was in a bit of a fog and things were turning a bit dramatic.

After the MRI I was asked to wait behind to see the doctors who wanted to talk to me. I was taken to an office where a junior doctor kept me company while we waited for two of her colleagues to join us. They showed me the images from the scans. This was the first time I saw the tumour. It was huge; the size of a small fist. The doctors explained the tumour could be cancerous. I did not properly hear what they were saying and kept thinking it was nothing. They asked me to listen carefully, to please listen to what they were saying; to prepare for the worst. I said it might not be cancer but they told me they were 99% sure.

They told me they would be referring me to Charing Cross Hospital and they would discuss my results with a Dr Stewart the next day. They gave me telephone numbers to ring if I was ill over night or if any radical changes occurred. I was still not scared; it just did not seem real. The weather was gorgeous. It was warm, the sun was shining and on the news we were told supermarkets were reporting record sales of ice cream, so it could not all be bad. Bad news should be accompanied by bad weather, rain, lightning and thunderstorms.

I took the bus back to Westbourne Grove where I quickly discovered having cancer was like owning a red car. Once you own a red car you suddenly notice how many red cars there are driving about. Everywhere you look you see red cars. I had never really noticed articles about cancer in newspapers and now I spotted two news stories about cancer on the journey home. One story was about a professor called Sanchia Aranda who told fellow Australians that it is important a cancer diagnosis is not hidden from children. They need to be told in a way that is appropriate to their age.

'All toddlers need to know is that mummy is going into hospital and she has a lump that needs to come out,' the professor advised. And Taylor Swift made a surprise visit to a thirteen year old super fan in a hospital in Brisbane, who had a bone cancer in her leg. I wondered if Bette Midler might surprise me with a visit to cheer me up should I need to go into hospital. Everything just seemed normal. It was time to tell one or two of my nearest and dearest that I might have cancer. But who would I tell first?

John and I have two adopted daughters. To say adopted is not entirely accurate. They are two of John's nieces and we have been close to them since they were little girls. They had always spent time with us on our annual trips to Ballyheigue and since they moved to London we have looked out for them. We are always telling them we cannot actually get rid of them. We tell them they have attached themselves to us and we are lumbered. The girls are twins and their names are Siobhan and Lisa. We have shared in their lives, approved or disapproved of their boyfriends, sang and danced at their weddings and were the first to see each of their four daughters. Lisa and I worked together for several years when I worked in the chemical industry. I guess that if you have to have a couple of limpets in your life, they might as well be these two wonderful creatures who would be the first to hear my news.

Siobhan's husband, Scott is a dentist. After our recent return from Ireland he looked at the swelling on my neck. I saw Scott throw a concerned look at Siobhan and I caught sight of his alarm, but he did not say anything. From that moment there were now four people who thought something more serious might be going on in my neck, Lisa Mc in Kinsale, Scott, Sandra and me. Scott told me weeks later he had been as worried as his sister-in-law in Kinsale.

Lisa is married to Kevin who after such scary news, decided I needed a treat and so he booked Lisa and me lunch at the Ivy in St Martins Lane. I love the Ivy; always have. Kevin could not get a table but this did not matter because we sat at the bar instead. The bar stalls are really comfortable and you get such a good view of the other diners. The barman was charming and looked after us royally. We Face Timed John in Bermuda. I could not confirm if I had cancer. The biopsy would tell us more. Having eaten liver and bacon, we had crème brûlée for afters.

We left the restaurant and decided to take a walk through Soho. We stopped for coffee at Bar Italia. This is something of a tradition with John and me. We always go for a coffee there if we have been to a party, out for dinner or the theatre in the area. Lisa and I sat outside and dodged the raindrops by sitting close up against the cafe's window and we tucked ourselves under the canopy. Lisa left to catch her train back home from Waterloo to Surbiton. I walked to John Lewis to have a look around. It seemed essential I carry on as usual doing normal things.

London has always been our playground. John and I live off the park near Queensway in Bayswater. We would not live anywhere else. Bayswater is probably one of the most cosmopolitan areas of London, which we love. It offers a wealth of distractions with its coffee shops, restaurants, and proximity to other areas and access to Hyde Park and Kensington Gardens. We often walk to Kensington High Street, Oxford Street, Knightsbridge and on a Saturday Portobello Road. But we have our freedom passes so we can go anywhere within the M25.

When John and I celebrated our civil partnership we shared the day with Lisa and Kevin and Siobhan and Scott. It was a great day. After the ceremony we had drinks and a snack in the Landmark Hotel, champagne in the Ritz and dinner in the Caprice. After the dinner we walked through Mayfair, where we finished off the day with drinks on the 28th floor of the Hilton Hotel on Park Lane. While we were waiting to go into the bar, a young camp guy carrying bags from expensive and exclusive shops flounced out with his lady companion.

'Where's my car. I want my car,' he shouted as he showed off by camping around the reception.

'Well, unless your car is Chitty, Chitty, Bang, Bang I guess it's downstairs in the road,' Kevin advised the punter who huffed, threw his head back and got in the lift and left. The guy on the door thanked us for getting rid of him and told us we had saved him the trouble of throwing out this customer, who had been a nuisance since he arrived.

When John and I went to Old Marylebone Town Hall to book the Yellow Room for our ceremony, we were interviewed by one of the registrars. His first job was to make sure we were not going to break the law and that our intentions were legitimate.

'Okay James,' he said. 'First things first; what's your full name please?'

'James Michael Kenny,' I answered.

'Really, not James Michael Holyfield?' he reminded me. 'Jumping ahead of yourself a bit aren't you James?' We all enjoyed my mistake and happily he later conducted the ceremony, which was just perfect.

'How long have you known each other and where did you meet?' the registrar asked us as he took notes.

John and I have been together since the first night we met on April 21st 1979. For over 38 years we have lived a wonderful life. I was twenty-seven when we met in a nightclub on Bond Street, which a few years later we helped run with a dear friend.

We make a great team. We have friends in Leamington Spa who we do not see so much anymore, but when we used to stay with them over a weekend they were always amazed how much we talked in the morning when we woke up. They could not believe what we found to talk about and it fascinated them. They would lay in their room listening to us happily chatting away in ours.

We come as a pair and people we know always use our two names in the same breath. It has been said time and time again that friends can never see one of us without the other one and they worry about what would happen if one of us died.

That is not to say we agree all the time and it would be true to say we can be fiery and the rows we have had in the past are legendary. Like the time in New York when we fell out in a club when a hunk flirted with John. We were dressed up because we had been to a posh restaurant. On the way back to our hotel we popped into a club when the shirtless hunk came onto John. John is a natural flirt and was flattered by the guy's attention. I knew John would not do anything out of line but I got annoyed when the hunk gave John a hug and he rubbed his sweaty skin on John's expensive suit. I could cope with the flirting because I knew the guy was wasting his time, but the body liquid made me furious. We had a row there at the bar and I left disgusted at what I had just witnessed. I got in a taxi, but this made John's night because he jumped into another cab and fulfilled a lifelong ambition when he shouted to the driver 'follow that cab'. The fact this happened in New York made it even more exciting.

Then there was the time I got so cross with him I threw a huge ashtray across the room as if it was a Frisbee and it stuck in the wall. John knows how to wind me up but we are also a great team and together we have built the life we like living. We do everything together and have the greatest circle of friends who we love to entertain in our little flat. John's family have adopted me as one of their own, which is why we love spending time in Ballyheigue at least once a year.

But more than anything John has been my rock. He supported me when I had difficult times at work and he gave me the confidence to take risks with my career, even when they might have impacted on our lives if they went wrong. There was the time when I was working at City and Guilds. I learned a lot and will always be grateful for the ideas I developed when working there. I always say it was where I did my apprenticeship and developed all my ideas about how education and training can best be provided. I was lucky to work there when it was a laboratory for ideas. Working in creative teams we developed programmes in collaboration with other organisations to help people learn in interesting and different ways outside boring classrooms. But over time I became frustrated and unhappy as new ideas were less encouraged.

At this time I heard of a new exciting job but it was on a year's contract. If I got the job I would be swopping the security of the current job with its pension and health care package for twelve months of excitement. John knew I was unhappy and told me to try for the new job. I got it and I went to enjoy being creative in a new and exciting environment, working for the chemical industry.

John supported me in everything. He accepted the long hours I worked and he put up with my short periods away from home traveling around the country running workshops and harvesting new ideas.

At the end of the twelve months I was offered a full time job. The salary was great. I had my own office in Westminster, a pension and health insurance, but even more importantly I was part of a great team doing exciting work with great employers and government departments. Leaving City and Guilds was scary but it worked. It worked because John believed in me.

The times ahead of us would strengthen our relationship even more and prove to the world how strong we are together.

After meeting Sandra, the x-ray, ultrasound, CT and an MRI scan I was now in the system. The NHS is wonderful when you are in their system. The trick is getting in. Painkillers and more painkillers cannot be the answer. I wondered why I had not met a Sandra before.

I had been to my GP several times with the same complaint and had even gone to accident and emergency in an ambulance back in December. I am convinced not having the MRI earlier caused further and possibly unnecessary problems and therefore extra expense. Had the tumour been discovered earlier the treatment may have been less complicated and therefore less expensive. I may have been spared the intrusive and brutal surgery that was to come.

Thursday loomed and my first meeting with Dr Stewart was only a sleep and a shower away. I decided I would take a notebook with me and I thought of some questions to ask him. Later I learned this was the best thing I could have done. It was important to keep notes because I would never have remembered everything I was told, especially when getting bad news, which can fuddle the brain. A note book kept me focused on what I was hearing and it helped me remain objective. Without my notebook

I am sure I would have been subjective and even hysterical. I took my notebook with me to all my meetings and consultations in London and America. Thankfully Meryl had agreed to come with me to the hospital. Howard and Pauline had told her to look after me.

I left home and travelled to Hammersmith on the 27 bus. I got there early and so I had time to walk around the area. I used to work on Fulham Palace Road and I wanted to see how it had changed. A few more cafes had opened and the area boasts a new park, but the changes were really minimal. Fringe Benefits, where I used to get my hair cut more than forty years ago was still there. I always thought that was such a great name for a hairdressing salon. It used to be owned by two gay guys. Hairdressers seem to be good at thinking up names for their shops. Headmasters, A Cut Above, Hair Today and Gone Tomorrow and Barber Streisand come to mind. The weather was gorgeous; warm and sunny. I had time to get a coffee, sit outside a café on Fulham Palace Road and watch the world go by. One of my greatest pleasures is to simply sit with a coffee and watch people going about their business.

It was time to go and meet Dr Stewart. The clinic had moved into temporary accommodation and it was not where the website had shown me it would be. It was a long walk to the back of the hospital. Meryl and I had arranged to meet at ten o'clock. I rang Meryl to tell her the clinic was not where I told her it would be, but her mobile went to answerphone. I made a mess of checking into the clinic. I tried to use the automated system, which I had not seen before and the receptionist was a bit abrupt with me. Humbled by the experience I took a seat in the waiting area and watched the different doctors and consultants call their patients. I wanted to know what each person had wrong with them. I had never met these people and so I made up what was wrong with them by their dress or the way they walked. From all the comings and goings I tried to work out which of the doctors was Dr Stewart.

Then he walked in, he was late and I was his first patient. No sign of Meryl. She must be lost. I went in and he asked me loads of questions about what had happened over the last thirteen months. He told me I would have blood tests and a biopsy that afternoon and we would meet again next week. I signed some consent forms and left. I went to reception where a really helpful guy booked another appointment for me to see Dr Stewart. I walked back down the long corridor when Meryl came round the corner. When she saw me she pretended to have climbed mountains and swam rivers to reach me. We sang 'River Deep, Mountain High' and did a quick dance. Poor Meryl had been all over the hospital looking for me. We hugged and laughed.

We never stopped talking. We gossiped about people and discussed their shortcomings in some detail, but we never once stopped to acknowledge our own faults of course. We do not have any. We were on a roll and enjoying our little world, we had no idea if other people in the hospital or the café could hear what we were talking about. We were having such a good time we probably did not even care. We only said good things about the people we love of course. We both agreed we had never really grown up. We still see the ridiculous side of life and are always surprised at how serious some people take themselves.

We are still quite juvenile and have a huge sense of fun. We laugh at stupid things and see humour in everything, even when there is only a tiny glimmer. We had learned it is foolish to spend time hating people because this takes up far too much energy and we agreed it was better to ignore people you do not like and spend your energy on the people you do. Hate is a horrible word anyway.

It was at this point I decided I would use the positive side of my personality to deal with any bad news I might get over the next week. Talking with Meryl helped me sort out my thoughts. When Meryl walked away to take a phone call, I thought about what we had been saying and there and then I decided I would react positively to any bad news coming my way.

Life is really just a series of events and experiences and of course some are good and others are bad. I have often wished I was a bit harder because sad or nasty events can affect me. But I am more likely to be affected by sad things that happen to other people close to me. I am much better at dealing with bad things that happen to me. But it would be some time before I got to know how my past experiences were to help me prepare for what I was going to have to face over the next twelve months.

I told Meryl a story about Lisa to explain how kind people could be. When my mother died Lisa and I were working together. Her colleagues told Lisa she must give me a call to see if I was okay. Lisa did not want to ring me. She procrastinated all morning. Then the moment came. The phone in our flat rang.

'Hello 6920.'

'Hi James this is Lisa. How's your mother?'

'She's dead Lisa.'

'I know but how is she?' I started laughing. Poor Lisa, I knew exactly what she was going through, she did not want to be put in this situation and because she is so kind she did not want to upset me.

I had my blood test and we went out to have lunch. On our return to the hospital we went and sat in the waiting area. We were called into a dark room for my biopsy. I took off my shirt and lay on a bed on my side. The lady doctor went for my neck. Assisted by a technician the doctor took five samples. It was horrible. When we left the hospital I felt awful. I felt weak and woozy and I wanted to be sick. I had to sit on a wall that surrounded a pond full of carp. I wobbled and Meryl stopped me from falling in. We joked that if she had not caught me, Pauline and Howard would have never forgiven her for letting me plop into a fish pond.

The journey home took us a bit of time. We had to walk slowly and had to stop for a coffee. We stopped at a shop to buy some painkillers. The pain was doubling me over. I lay on the bed and Meryl stayed for an hour to keep me company. The biopsy had really hurt. Later that evening when I was on my own and the pain did not look like it was going away anytime soon, the horrific news of the terror attack in Nice came through where eighty six people were murdered and four hundred and fifty eight people were injured on Bastille Day. I felt strangely sad and vulnerable. Thank goodness John was able to return home from Bermuda on the Sunday. I needed more than ever to see him. His employer, who is a great friend, has been so understanding and marvellous through this whole horrible experience. She has been kind, generous and supportive.

As arranged I went back to see Dr Stewart a week later for the results of the biopsy. Judgement day had arrived. John and I took the 27 bus and again the weather was glorious. I pointed out Fringe Benefits but I do not think John was interested. He was too worried and deep in his thoughts about what we might hear. Dr Stewart called us in. He was charming and broke the news very sympathetically.

He told us I had a rare form of bone cancer; a Chordoma pronounced kor-doh-mer. This was the first time I had heard the word Chordoma and over the next few weeks I was going to have trouble with it. It did not sound that bad. I thought it sounded more like a fast food you might pop in to buy on the way home after a boozy night out.

'Oh, let me see. What will I have? Oh yes give me a Chordoma please.'

'Do you want chips and salad with that?'

'Yes please, but only salad and no dressing, I'm on a diet.'

'Right okay, that'll be £6.82 please. Anything for your friend?'

Dr Stewart is a throat specialist and explained he would not be able to do the surgery. He told us he would need to refer me to another hospital as Charing Cross did not have the necessary expertise. He said he would make some calls to see what would be the best course of action. My reaction to his news was weird. I wanted to argue with him and plead with him to do the operation right there and then. I did not want this to go on and on. I was convinced he was being modest or telling lies and in my confusion I was sure he could help me.

I had often thought about how I might react to such huge bad news, just as I had imagined what I would do with the money if I ever won the lottery or received an unexpected inheritance. For years I had rehearsed my reactions in my head during quiet moments on trains and buses, or when I laid in bed waiting to fall asleep. I had imagined myself being in total control or screaming hysterically, but I had never visualised the panic of the weird and the confused.

My forehead felt like it was swelling out in front of me so it could hold all the horrible information my poor old brain was being asked to compute. In those few short seconds I experienced something like a migraine, a blood rush, a knock on the head and several panic attacks. My head stopped spinning, things began to slow down and over a few seconds I became coldly rational and calm. I began to make a little sense of what was happening. I now saw the raw pain of being eaten by cancer. The meeting broke up and John walked away. I stayed back and taking my time I asked Dr Stewart if I was in trouble.

'Big trouble,' he told me.

'Is there anything I can do? What advice would you give me?' I asked him.

'If I was you, I would go home and tell everybody,' he told me. 'Tell everyone you know. Family, friends, neighbours and work colleagues. You may not hear from some people. Those who won't be able to cope with your news will keep quiet, but others will be there for you.' He also said I would need all the support I could muster. How right he was and what a great piece of advice it turned out to be. He explained that if I did not tell everybody those I left out might take offence. This was no time to upset people, unlike Mr Donald Trump I thought, who must have upset Hilary Clinton when he accepted the Republican nomination for President by giving a seventy five minute speech in which he accused her 'death, destruction, terrorism and weakness.'

We went home on a quiet and eerie 27 bus and I rang people. I told my sister who thanked God our parents were not alive. She thought the news would destroy them. When I was awarded the MBE back in 2013 she said it was a pity they were not alive because they would have been so proud. I sent a detailed email to other people I see regularly:

Dear Friends

Apologies for sending you an email. I would have preferred to meet you for a drink or speak on the 'phone, but I have had to tell so many people my news my ear is phone tired! I have some bad news I'm afraid. There is no way to really dress this up so here we go - I have a very rare form of cancer. But do not worry; I'm being really positive about this and doctors tell me there are some good things in my favour. Apparently, I'm slim, healthy and fit which all helps and I'm going to the Charing Cross hospital which is a centre of excellence.

I've been having tests for the last four weeks. Finally, I had a biopsy which confirmed I have what is called a Chordoma tumour. These are very rare and only occur in one in a million people. It is attached to my spine in my neck. The fact it is rare is also good because everyone is interested in what treatment to give me. This was all confirmed last Thursday and we are now waiting to hear what the doctors will do.

Anyway I hope all is well with you and you are enjoying what you can from this sad old summer. But we had three glorious weeks in Ireland. The weather was unbelievable. We also went around Scotland on the Royal Caledonian in May for five days. This luxury train was a great experience but we ate so much. The food was amazing and we met some really interesting people.

Lots of love

James

xxx

Writing the email actually helped me compartmentalise the issues and I filed all the bits of what I had been told away in my head.

The pain had grown steadily worse over the months, but now it was really bad and over the next two weeks it was going to get even worse. This was to be my life for the next nine weeks, where I would spend most of my days lying on the bed in pain. I did make myself go out and I would keep appointments at the hospital but life was getting more and more difficult. I could not travel far and I missed the Sunday club lunch when it was Meryl's turn to host. The last two weeks of July were terrible but I was determined to do as much as I could and we did make it to a friend's barbecue where I told the guests I had cancer. They were all great and offered to help by running me to my appointments.

We were in Scott and Siobhan's garden on the last Sunday in July with a couple of their friends who were over from Ireland for the weekend. It had been a challenge to drive the car but we made it and just to pile on the pressure I got a parking ticket that day. We were eating a barbecue and John started telling one of his hilarious stories. The only problem is, John can digress and not keep to the point, which in itself can be funny. He adds and adds. We always joke that he does not exactly embroider a story, but is more likely to crochet a tale.

'Excuse me John,' I said to interrupt him. 'You do know I have cancer don't you? If you don't hurry up and finish the story I might not be around to hear the ending.' Everybody thought this was both wicked and hilarious. This was the first time I understood the best way to face the future, in addition to being positive was with humour; even outrageous or shocking humour.

But August was a washout and I spent most of the time lying on the bed hoping the pain, which I was sure had been made worse by the biopsy would go away. But no matter what happens there always seems to be someone somewhere in the world who is worse off, like the one hundred and fifty nine people who were killed and the others who were injured and made homeless in the Italian earthquake, where half of all the beautiful one thousand year old buildings in the village of Amatrice were destroyed.

But there was news worth celebrating from the Rio Olympics when Team GB came second in the medals table ahead of China. It cheered me up that, not since the modern Olympic era began in 1896, had a country increased its medal tally at the summer Games immediately following one it hosted, where we went from winning sixty five medals in London to sixty seven in Rio.

Dr Stewart was right the love that came back was incredible.

Emails started coming in and get well cards arrived for months. People I had not seen for years started to get in touch because they heard what was happening to me through other friends who kept in touch using social media such as Facebook. During August I was in regular telephone contact with Scott's mother Lynn. Lynn had had cancer for months now and was getting weaker. We helped each other by comparing notes and we took strength from what was happening to us. We even managed to cheer each other up and always ended the telephone call with laughter using what to other people would be black humour. I rang Lynn one Friday and she said she was too weak to talk. She was exhausted and was waiting for the doctor. Lynn died the next day.

The next few months up to Christmas were totally different to anything I had experienced before. I stayed in the flat during August, spent time in and out of hospital during September and early October and spent time back in the flat during November and December. My freedom pass took a holiday and I missed my shopping trips, lunch dates and visits to the theatre. Not going to Portobello Road on a Saturday became symbolic of what was going on. John and I decided a visit to Portobello Road would be something to aim for.

I did go out to attend hospital appointments. But this was a struggle. And every time a friend rang or visited we always talked about the cancer. Cancer now defined me. I always tried to change the subject when in a conversation but the tumour always got its way and somehow managed to make itself the centre of attention, which was odd because it had hidden for months but was now out of the closet it wanted to show off.

I wondered what friends and I had talked about before the tumour had been discovered living in my neck. Now everybody wanted dates and details about what would happen. Everybody constantly asked me how I felt. 'Was I okay?' I always answered I was fine, because I was. I still had the pain of course but nothing radical had developed yet and thankfully nothing had fallen off. I remained positive and looked forward to the future now I knew what I had.

In order to understand more about what was happening to me; I decided to get to know my tumour. I was going to cope with the news by giving the tumour an identity, a name, a personality and a history so I could visualise it. Over time I would develop a relationship with it so I could happily see it killed off.

During the time I laid on the bed in August I created Dolores Tumour. I told myself Dolores Tumour had taken up residence about eighteen months ago. She moved in on her own accord. I neither asked nor invited her to stay rent free. She simply squatted and used up my resources. Her family name was Tumour, but because of her ambition to sound more worldly and sophisticated, the disillusioned Dolores pronounced it Toomoore.

Dolores Toomoore lived in my neck where she had attached herself to my spine. Dolores had been a showgirl in Las Vegas. She had never made the big time. She had danced in second rate bars off the main strip for pin money, which sometimes only paid for her food. She never had sufficient funds to properly sustain herself. Her face showed what a tough life she had had. From across a room she could pass off as something nearly presentable, but up close the lines that could be seen through her cracked makeup told another story. There was nothing subtle about Dolores; she was all tits, teeth and feathers. Life had been tough on Dolores. Her silver sling backs were well worn. The leather was cracked and elastic stretched. Above the shoes the back of her thighs were pitted with cellulite. Her badly bleached hair was brittle from the over use of cheap hair dyes bought from unreliable internet sites. Men had treated her badly and on occasions had taken advantage of the soft side of her character.

Over the years she had grown bitter, even ruthless. She had to survive at any cost. She was angry at what life had dealt her. She was bitter that Mr Right had not come her way and for all the Mr Wrongs that had. She had given her heart away to pigs and had paid the price.

She hated having to live in apartments which although cheap she could not easily afford. She was a wicked old frump. I could not feel sorry for her. I hated her living in me and off me. She was eating my spine for free. Why should I feel sorry for an old bitch that had made all the wrong life choices and who had not even finished high school in some old boring mid-west USA town? I was now ready to have Dolores evicted. Dolores had to go; she deserved to be destroyed. It was either her or me and it was not going to be me.

On some days, when I thought about how horrible Dolores could be, I would think of her even more unpleasant and dreary cousin called Dolorous, the bringer of pain and sorrow who was grievous and mournful.

3. Informed

'The British nation is unique in this respect: they are the only people who like to be told how bad things are, who like to be told the worse.'

Winston Churchill

The last week of July and the first three weeks of August were a desert of information. I now knew Dolores was squatting in my neck, she had unpacked, set up home and decided to stay. But I did not know what was going to happen to get rid of her. Dr Stewart had promised to make some calls so I could be referred to someone who had the expertise to help me, but I had heard nothing. Dolores must have thought she was getting away with murder; perhaps she actually was.

Then out of the blue I got a phone call from Charing Cross Hospital. An extremely polite and helpful young lady asked me if I had heard from the National Hospital for Neurology and Neurological Surgery in Queen's Square. I told her I had not. As no one had contacted me she promised to chase them and she went on to explain that Dr Stewart had referred me to the National because he thought it was the best place for someone with my type of cancer. She promised to get back to me but a little later someone from the National phoned me about an appointment to attend a clinic on Friday at 09.45. I was to see Dr Vittorio Russo. This level of service impressed me enormously and I made sure to tell everybody who contacted me how impressed I was.

In the meantime Neil and Scott, who did not know I had been referred to the National, each did some research into who might be best placed to look after me. As coincidence would have it, they both honed in on a surgeon called Mr David Choi who is based at the National. As Dr Stewart had referred me to the same hospital, I hoped Mr Choi would take up the case. I later found out Mr Choi was on annual leave.

Neil and Nichola came over on Friday to take us for my first appointment with Mr Russo. They did not want us to travel by bus, tube or taxi and insisted on taking us. All our friends were being marvellous. During the consultation Dr Russo told us nine facts about what would happen, which I listed in my trusty note book:

1. Mr David Choi would probably lead the team looking after me.
2. It will take time to sort out my treatment because two teams are involved, where neurosurgeons will remove the tumour and oncologists will deal with the cancer through for example the use of radiotherapy. But first they have to agree if radiotherapy would help before going ahead with surgery.
3. The spine is stable, which was very good news.
4. The tumour had grown around a main artery.
5. The head of the oncology team will be Dr Beatrice Seddon who is a colleague of Mr Choi.
6. The operation will take all day.
7. I will get better.
8. The team will remove the tumour.
9. My recovery time will be about six to eight weeks.

Mr Russo showed us all the images from the CT and MRI scans and I realised that, although I had not heard from them, huge amounts of work had taken place discussing my case. The news was a bit scary but all very positive. Another appointment with Mr Russo was booked for next week following a meeting of the two teams who would finalise the stages they will use to evict Dolores. Mr Russo could see I was in pain, but asked me to bear with it for a bit longer because I was already on strong medication.

My second appointment with Mr Russo was a bit more exciting. The patient before me was a prisoner. We knew this because he was wearing chains and was accompanied by two well-built handsome prison officers. I did not know people were still put in chains and it looked so old fashioned and out of place. The corridor was very narrow and it was a bit scary.

After his visit with Mr Russo, the officers let the prisoner use the toilet. We wondered if they had checked to see if the toilet had windows and we hoped we were witnessing a prison break. But sadly nothing that dramatic happened. Either the toilet did not have windows or perhaps the prisoner was not that adventurous after all. Either way he went peacefully. I was quite disappointed because I had hoped the prisoner would try to escape, but perhaps he was feeling poorly and just not up to it. We did think it a bit much that we had to pay for our own taxi to and from the hospital, compared to the prisoner who got his transport covered by the taxpayer; plus he was accompanied by two well-built handsome men.

During my second meeting, Mr Russo confirmed Mr Choi had taken on my case; which would be a cause for Neil, Scott and me to open a bottle or two.

We heard this good news on the day the NHS looked like it was in for a tough time with warnings in the press about obesity and failing to complete heart checks.

To point out the dangers of the country sleep walking into an obesity crisis, the BBC were due to show a ground breaking documentary about a post-mortem examination of an obese woman that showed the impact of fat on a person's organs.

A report by MPs and charities also claimed that one third of hospitals in England were failing to roll out a simple £28 health check for identifying potential heart failure. But there was some good news; another report recommended cancer patients be given cannabis.

The week running up to my meeting with Mr Choi seemed to take forever. For someone who had been in hundreds of meetings during his working life, I was impatient to have the most important meeting of my life; a meeting where I would meet people who were to become our heroes and for whom we have the greatest respect and admiration.

Mr Choi introduced us to Michelle. Michelle was responsible for organising my treatment and tracking my progress. Michele would agree dates, book operating theatres and make sure various staff were available at critical moments. I could not begin to realise what a difficult and complex job Michelle had working with and coordinating so many different experts. I could not fully understand what Michelle had to do, but I totally appreciated what she was doing for me.

We thought the meeting was simply to meet Mr Choi, but all hell broke loose. He went through some of the risks associated with the surgery. He told me the operation came with considerable dangers where I might not walk again; I might lose my voice and not be able to control my bladder, which would mean me having to be fitted with a colostomy bag. I asked him if I could die and he said yes, so I told him not to tell me anything else.

He also told me a spinal team made up of experts from several hospitals had been discussing my case and they were confident they now had all the information to perform the operations to remove this huge tumour successfully. Dolores had put on a lot of weight. Following the surgery Dr Beatrice Sneddon would plan my radiotherapy and possibly also proton beam therapy to kill off any remaining cells. I would need two operations which would be massive and surgically intrusive, but Mr Choi said he would make me better and give me my life back. He sounded so confident he raised my spirits. I just knew I was in good hands. I would also need to have a nuclear scan to make sure I did not have other tumours lurking somewhere in my body.

'When do we start all this?' I asked.

'Tomorrow. You need to be here early in the morning for the first preparatory operation.' Crikey, I thought this was too quick. My first operation would be with a Mr Robertson who would isolate a main artery in my neck so the big operations to evict Dolores could happen on later dates. Michelle told me she had been organising all my operations. This turned out to be a massive logistical exercise because of the complexity of what was going to happen. Michelle had been working on this for weeks. Coordinating events, booking operating theatres, anaesthetists and other surgeons able to support Mr Choi who had also been liaising with a team based in Stanmore. The operations would only go ahead if an ear, nose and throat surgeon is available to support Mr Choi. I had no idea this had been happening while I was lying on my bed thinking I had been lost in the system.

'One last question if I may. Do I have to have the operations and the radiotherapy?' I asked. I wanted to know if it was safe to leave Dolores where she was; or at least how long she could be left untreated.

'No you don't have to have the operations. That is up to you of course. You will need to sign the consent papers.'

'Phew, thank goodness for that. That's a relief,' I said.

'But if you leave it, we estimate you'll be dead by Christmas. Your tumour is particularly aggressive and it is big. You don't really have much choice,' Mr Choi told me.

'Bloody hell,' I replied. 'In that case let's get on with it. I'll see you in the morning. Please don't tell me anymore. I promise to be a good boy.'

I felt strangely optimistic about the whole thing. This was going to be the biggest challenge of my life and I was going to make the most of it. I wanted to see if I could do this. I did not care what deal Dolores had done with Dr Death, they were not going to win this one. Michelle told me what would happen, which I added to my notebook:

1. September 13th - Isolate third artery
2. September 16th - Nuclear testing to see if I have any other tumours
3. September 21st - Fit feeding tube in stomach
4. September 27th - Pre operation assessment
5. September 28th - First operation to remove Chordoma
6. October 5th   - Second operation to remove Chordoma
7. October   - Possible period of radiotherapy

The pages of my little black notebook were filling up. We went home shell shocked and a little bit bewildered. As I explained before, one of the great things about having John is that when something like this happens we talk about it and make sense of everything. We went over what Mr Choi had told us and thought about tomorrow's event. I sent another email:

Dear Friends

Since my follow up appointment with Mr Russo last week the hospital has pulled out all the stops and loads of things have been happening behind the scenes. And so it begins......

I return to the hospital tomorrow for an operation to isolate one of my main arteries which is surrounded by the tumour. I will be in hospital until the weekend.

1. *On September 21st I will be fitted with a feeding tube because after the two main operations I will not be able to eat normally.*
2. *On September 28th I will have the first operation to remove part of the tumour.*
3. *On or around October 5th I will have the second operation to remove the rest of the tumour. A third operation may be necessary.*
4. *Mr David Choi is now in charge and he said that although I will have a tough time I will get better.*

*5. My post op oncology treatment will be managed by Dr
Seddon and I may have to travel abroad. The whole
process is likely to take six months. The NHS is fantastic.*

*The meeting today was really scary; I have left out some of the
gory detail, but the treatment I am getting is of a gold standard.
The team is amazing and Mr Choi is the best in the UK for this type
of treatment.*
We hope you are all well.
Love
John and James
xxx

I went to bed quite calm and reflected on what was happening
and what had happened to me. The battle had begun.

Being told you have cancer is devastating because it changes
your life so much. People react in different ways. The English can
joke and try to make light of it and I discovered later that while
Americans are better informed about the risks and what may
happen, they turn to God for help.

I decided I would do what the doctors told me and I now knew
surgery, followed by a course of chemotherapy and or
radiotherapy would be the best way to deal with Dolores. It was
time to be practical and face up to what needed to be done.

It was so important to be well informed about my diagnosis and
to fully accept what was happening to me. Armed with this
knowledge I could be serious and adopt an approach that was
more likely to help me get better. I was going to need all my
willpower to get through this.

By being well informed about my choices I knew exactly what the
doctors had to do and how I could help them. Nothing else would
do. I had to be practical. Relying on God or humour or even both
might help me deal with what was going on, but they would not
cure me. I would have to go under the knife and get myself
zapped. I decided to take on that hard-nosed bitch Dolores and
throw all I could at her. I would use the humour to harden my

resolve and stop me from wallowing in self-pity. No time for self-pity; far too busy getting the job done. I would also have a comforting word with God now and then during quiet peaceful moments. I remembered I did not have to have the surgery. It was my choice. But if I elected not to have the operations, I would be dead by Christmas; probably.

I fell asleep thinking about Dolores. I was beginning to find out more about her and although we had only recently met, I was learning fast about how ruthless, selfish and tricky she could be.

4. Surgery

'If the operation is difficult, you are not doing it properly'

Alberto Pena

The alarm woke me. It was Tuesday. I had to be at the hospital by eight o'clock to get ready for Mr Robinson. John and I are not used to getting up early and we had got into the habit of sleeping for longer since I had retired. We took life much more slowly these days and worked hard to avoid early mornings. When we went to Ireland we drove to Wales the night before the ferry crossing so we did not have to get up when it was still dark and make that mad dash down the M4 to catch the boat. We did not do early morning flights anymore either. It now seems silly to get to Gatwick or Stansted in time for an early flight, just to get a cheaper deal or add a few precious extra hours to a two week holiday. For the sake of a few quid we had made the conscious decision to reduce as many stresses as we could.

We went to reception and were told to go upstairs to the Victor Horsley Surgery Preparation Ward. Crikey, what a mouthful; I had trouble remembering it; I prayed we would find it. I was not nervous; I was more excited with anticipation. I had never been in hospital for a serious operation before where I would actually stay in a ward and be nursed back to health or perhaps even die. This was all new to me and I was beginning to find the whole experience interesting.

My knowledge of hospitals was limited, where I had only ever been an outpatient several times to sort out a bit of sciatica, to have tests to be told I have vertigo, which over the years had made me deaf in my left ear and I had had a growth removed from my forehead at Charing Cross and follow-up consultations with a dermatologist at St Mary's in Paddington every three months for two years.

One particular consultation was embarrassing but hilarious. Sometimes I would arrive to find my doctor was not there and I would see an Australian doctor instead. I really liked this doctor because she was so friendly and had the best Australian accent I had ever heard. It was loud and a bit brittle.

'Okay James. You know the drill. Get behind the screen and get your kit off,' she told me in the jolly accent. Then she added. 'Would you mind if three students sat in on the consultation today James?'

Working in education and training I knew trainees had to practice. 'No problem. Yes of course,' I answered.

I removed my jeans and wished I did not work in education and training. I might have refused. I stepped out from behind the screen in my underpants to see my doctor and three beautiful young Asian women standing there holding magnifying glasses. I stood on the spot in the middle of the room where they would get the best view. The doctor turned on the three spotlights pointing at me. There was no going back now and under these lights there was no hiding place. They surrounded me and on cue advanced towards me brandishing their magnifying glasses with obvious relish. I was to be examined to an inch of my dignity. I held in my tummy and squeezed my eyes shut. I did not hear a word they were saying to each other; I could only hear the loud pitched noise of panic in my head. But I did hear the doctor say what I was dreading.

'Are you alright James?' I nodded yes. 'Good on ya. Okay, time to lose the pants?' I opened my eyes and pushed them to the floor where they sat on my ankles. It got worse.

'Okay James, grab your knees,' she told me. No crease or crevice was left unexamined. I sat on the table and they even looked between my toes. My private bits had completely disappeared; they ran away and hid out of complete embarrassment. My session was over, I dressed and made a promise to join a gym.

We found the Victor Horsley Surgery Preparation Ward and were shown into a reception area. We were the first to be seen. After a little while a couple of other people arrived. I found out later that Wednesday is the main day for operations, not Tuesdays. During the morning I began to meet various members of staff who over the next couple of months would become friends. A junior doctor asked us to follow him through to the preparation area. I was given a bed behind blue curtains. He told me I would meet Mr Robinson shortly, be asked to sign consent papers and be prepared for the operation. He left and John and I sat waiting. We agreed John would go back to reception when Mr Robertson arrived. It seemed like ages before he came in.

Mr Robertson took me through what would happen. Dolores was growing around one of the arteries which Mr Choi needed isolated and blocked so he could remove Dolores safely. Mr Robertson would use dye to make sure the other arteries were healthy. Closing down this third artery would be permanent but he assured me I could live quite happily with the other three. I prayed he was right. I still had everything I had arrived with and I was reluctant to lose anything, even my appendix. Mr Robertson explained there was a risk I could have a stroke. But he assured me that twenty five other people had had this operation before me and only one lady had suffered a stroke, which turned out to be minor and she recovered after twenty four hours. Ummhhh. Was this one of my nine lives? I signed the consent papers and there was no turning back.

The junior doctor and a nurse came in to help me get ready for surgery. I told them this was all new to me and they promised to explain what was going on. They had a surgical gown and horrible long white socks, which were a bit of an effort to get on. They told me Mr Robertson was an excellent surgeon. I undressed.

'Are you really sixty three?' one of them asked me.

'Yes, afraid so,' I replied.

'Blimey,' he said. 'I hope I look like you when I'm old. You have a great body.' Old; I did not feel old.

'Thanks. I have been going to the gym for a few years now, but not since July because of the pain in my neck. But I have lost quite a bit of weight recently.' I was a bit surprised by the compliment but also flattered.

A little later I was wheeled down to the operating theatre where I met my anaesthetist. We got on very well. He asked about my work and I told him I was retired. He said he envied me and explained that he was counting the days to his retirement. He had downloaded an App on his mobile phone which recorded his retirement date. As each day passed the App deleted that day from the total, so he always knew how many days he had left to work. He loved his job but was really disappointed about what the government was doing to the NHS. He did not believe the government appreciated what we have or how precious the NHS is. I was shocked that such a highly trained and skilled man who actually loved his job would be counting off the days to his retirement? We talked about the Health Minister and wondered what word rhymed nicely with Hunt. I fell asleep saying the rhyming word out loud.

I woke in a bed on the Bernard Stanley Ward. I could not feel a thing and felt great. John was waiting for me. The operation had not gone ahead. On the advice of Mr Robertson, Mr Choi had cancelled the operation. The risks had been too great. They had feared a severe stroke. During the operation Mr Robertson had discovered my throat and oesophagus were seriously damaged. The problems I had had with reflux over the years had left an impressive mark. Years of a scorched earth policy by my digestive system had left me with significant burn tissues. I was turning out to be a bit of a medical miracle, a medical curiosity, a medical peculiar. I was adding to my list of complaints.

Michelle later told me Mr Choi was thinking of other ways of removing Dolores without damaging the artery. The procedure would be more complex but I was in the hands of the best team in England. Dolores was proving to be a tricky old cow. She had wrapped herself around my spine and was chomping away at my bones. Dolores was now obese and seemed to be growing by the day. Unlike me, I was losing weight. I had lost over fourteen pounds in a month. But this did not seem to worry my surgical team, who thought being fit and healthy was more important. Dolores had damaged the bones and was now compromising the integrity of my spine.

I stayed in hospital overnight to help me get over the anaesthetic and this is when I discovered how good the food was in the National. I had beef stew with dumplings for dinner. I could have eaten a couple more of those gorgeous dumplings. My only complaint had to be with the apple juice, the National did not run to wine, which was my only disappointment. So my day had not turned out to be as bad as I thought it might have been and I still had all my main arteries and I had been spared a stroke. Unlike Mr David Cameron, who had had a bad day when he announced his resignation as MP for Witney.

I found the ward really cosy and peaceful and had a great night's sleep. I was beginning to think staying in hospital in the future was not going to be as bad as I had imagined. I went home the next morning.

From now on my life was to be spent travelling backwards and forwards to hospitals. They were to become a way of life.

My next visit was to University College London Hospital, UCLH to have a nuclear scan to make sure I was free from other tumours. We wanted to make sure Dolores was travelling alone. The last thing I wanted to find out was that a couple of her dance troupe had travelled with her.

The following week would see me checked back into the National so I could be fitted with a feeding tube. I would not be able to swallow food after the second cancer operation and would be fed glorified milk shakes through a tube direct into my stomach. Feeding me using a tube up my nose would not be an option because of the surgery to my throat. We had a quiet time at home over the next few days and John prepared some lovely meals. I was eating loads but still losing weight.

The radioactive scan confirmed I did not have other tumours. This was a relief. Dolores had travelled alone or perhaps she was barren and unable to have children. Thank goodness for her life of late nights, hard liquor, fags and drugs; not to mention her poor choice in men.

I went back into the National for my pre-assessment in advance of having the feeding tube fitted. I was put in a single private room on the Molly Lane Fox Ward. The plan was for me to stay in one night and to have the feeding tube fitted through my stomach the next day. I ended up staying for three nights. I met Ernest who assisted Mr Choi. He was the gentlest and most considerate American I had ever met. He was so kind and always took me through what would happen during each procedure. He agreed to telephone John after each operation to tell him I was okay.

The operation would not be performed at the National but in the Gastronomic Department at UCLH. This meant I had to be transported across to UCLH in an ambulance accompanied by a nurse so the ward was missing a key member of staff during this time.

The first attempt to fit the tube failed because the surgeon discovered my stomach, bladder and colon were not where they should be. All my insides were mixed up, which suggested perhaps I was an alien. He would need more information on where to make the incision. He did not want to pierce my bladder, which I was assured would be particularly nasty. I returned to the National where an MRI had been quickly arranged to discover where to make the incision safely. I returned to UCLH again the next day in an ambulance and accompanied by my friendly nurse.

The second attempt to fit the tube also failed because although I had had the MRI, the radiologist failed to mark with a felt tip pen where the surgeon should make the incision. I returned to the National.

The third attempt to fit the tube was cancelled because someone did not order a dye which I was supposed to swallow so the surgeon could see where to make the incision with the help of a resident radiologist. In America there were also cancellations where Hilary Clinton cancelled her planned visit to riot torn Charlotte at the request of the mayor following the shooting of an African American by Charlotte police.

It took some time to return to the National. No ambulances were available. My nurse and I sat in the lobby of UCLH. I was now seriously pissed off. If the tube was not fitted, the first major operation scheduled for Wednesday would not go ahead. I lost it. I got angry and insisted we walk back to the National by going up Gower Street and through Bloomsbury. I would have looked a fine sight in my slippers and hospital issue pyjamas. But I did have on a warm cardigan. I just wanted to get back. The nurse struggled with me for a bit before I calmed down. I hated myself and kept apologising to the nurse because I could not believe I had been a nuisance to her. We made it back safely in an ambulance; a bit chilled but safely.

Back in my bed in the warm I felt much better. I was reading my book when the door flew open. The ward sister filled the frame. She was not a large woman, but her temper must have made her swell. She spoke. Her voice was low, tightly controlled but her anger was obvious and I thought she might explode.

'Mr Holyfield, I'm sorry you do not have the tube. I'm really sorry you don't have the tube. But heads will roll. Trust me Mr Holyfield heads will roll. I will NOT have my nurses off the ward all day and I will NOT be mucked about like this Mr Holyfield. Heads will roll Mr Holyfield, heads will roll I'm telling you.' She turned and disappeared.

A nurse came in and told me I could go home for the weekend. John was in Leigh-on-Sea at Lynn's funeral. I rang John but could not get him so I rang Siobhan and then Lisa to explain what had happened. All their phones went to voicemail. So I dressed and packed. I did regret missing my dinner because I had ordered the beef stew with the dumpling. I rang Siobhan again who told John the procedure had failed. He was really upset for me. I told him I would return to the National on Monday, the tube would be fitted on Tuesday and I would see back at the flat. The nurses told me to have a good weekend and I went home by taxi.

I unpacked and was glad to see our little flat. I was sorry to have missed Lynn's funeral but John told me how beautiful it had been. Scott had organised a lovely lunch in a restaurant overlooking the beach in honour of his mother. We had had some great times in Leigh-on-Sea over the years. Lynn had a beautiful garden and the town itself is charming with its great shops and restaurants. By Christmas the house was sold and my links with Leigh were severed. I was going to miss Lynn deeply. No more lunches on the High Street.

On the Saturday Siobhan and Scott brought their friends Debra and Eunan round for a visit. They had come over from Ireland for Lynn's funeral. We have known Debra for years. We met her when she had shared a flat with Siobhan and Lisa in Tralee and she is another one of our adopted daughters. We had been to her wedding and when she had her hen weekend in London we had thrown a brunch for her in the flat on the Sunday before she left to go back to Dublin where she lived. On this particular occasion we caused a security scare at Stansted. Debra was going through security and something particularly suspicious was spotted in her carry-on bag. She could not think what it might be and the security men went into meltdown. As a precaution Debra and her bag were both isolated. Her bag was opened and they discovered the leftover sausages and bacon from the brunch which I had wrapped twice in aluminium foil.

Debra was her usual bright and cheerful self. Debra is a lovely person who knows how to have a great time. When she and Eunan celebrated their 10th wedding anniversary, Eunan organised an amazing party in a castle in Ireland. Twelve of us met in the bar and surprised Debra when she walked in. The meal on the Saturday night was one of the best meals I have ever had.

For an anniversary present we found an unusual honeypot in an auction. Eunan was building his family a new house with an enormous kitchen and we thought the honeypot an ideal gift. It was in the shape of a bee. It had a glass body for the honey and silver legs, face and wings. A friend who sells unusual and expensive glass and bone china, told us these honeypots rarely come on the market because they are usually given as keepsakes to guests who attend royal weddings. On the underside of the wings was the crest of the Spanish Royal Family. We like finding unusual presents that people would never buy themselves.

During their visit to the flat Siobhan told me I was too thin. I agreed but said I could not do much about it. I told Siobhan she was a great person to have around when not feeling too well. A real pick-me-up she is. I think Siobhan enjoyed the joke, but I always love Siobhan's honesty.

On Monday I returned to the hospital for my first big week. I was checked into the Bernard Stanley ward. Howard and Meryl visited me. Howard told me he had been talking to a friend in Dallas who was a surgeon. This surgeon had told Howard I was in the best place and under the best team in the world for these types of cancer. I did not doubt it.

Before I could have the first big operation on Wednesday to sort out Dolores there was still the business of fitting the tube so I could be fed and nourished. On Tuesday morning Ernest came to see me. He reassured me that they had to get it right today and was sure the operation would be successful. A lot was at stake and we were cutting it fine.

I was taken from the National to UCLH by ambulance lying down in my bed and thinking how silly I must have looked I giggled. I had swallowed the blue dye. This time nothing was being left to chance. When I was wheeled into the operating theatre I was surprised to see what was going on. The surgeon was going to be assisted by two radiographers who had the job of telling him how to avoid my bladder. There were four surgeons altogether.

Three had come to observe the little alien whose insides were round the wrong way. One had travelled all the way from Reading.

They asked my permission to stay and I agreed. I knew how important it is for people to keep learning and expanding their knowledge. I had after all stood naked under bright lights in front of an Australian lady and three young beautiful Asian women armed with magnifying glasses. How bad could an operation be? Several nurses were busy getting the room and me ready. My surgeon told me Mr Choi had threatened him if he did not get this procedure right. They were all asked to put on safety aprons and the procedure began. The last I remember was seeing them all looking at my insides on two large screens and talking about what they were going to do. Sleep.

The procedure took much longer than normal. Apparently it should only last about thirty minutes. I was out for over an hour and a half. I woke to find my second visitor had moved in, but I could not bring myself to look at it. I did not want to see what it looked like. I decided having a pipe hanging out of my stomach could not be a good look. It's not the sort of thing you would wear to a beach.

Lying in the ambulance on my journey back to the National, I thought about the feeding tube. One or two people I had met over the last week had described the tube as a peg so I called it Peggy Fry. I decided she had been a cook in an old boys' public school. She was chubby, ruddy cheeked and she had fat pink hands. She had been a mother to all the boys in the school and had been known to dish out harmless medicines when the boys felt homesick or slightly poorly. Poor old Peggy was a nice old soul who would soon be retired. She was a spinster and was looking forward to moving back to live near her older sister in an old cathedral city in East Anglia. Now we were on speaking terms I was not so concerned about old Peggy and I felt around to see what she felt like. It was just a soft plastic tube.

When I was settled back in, Pauline came to visit and while we were chatting Mr Choi came to brief me about what was going to happen the next day. Much later Pauline told me she had observed how well Mr Choi and I seemed to get on. It appeared we had developed an understanding and professional relationship to the point where I fully trusted him and he appreciated my positivity and determination to get better.

I had beef with dumpling for dinner because I liked it so much. I slept really well, which surprised me. I thought I would lay awake all night worrying. I thought about this next morning. I could not exactly put my finger on why I slept so well. Perhaps it was because I knew I was in good hands and felt so confident with my surgery team I had nothing to worry about? Perhaps I was really an alien and therefore feared nothing? Perhaps I was just thick and a bit stupid? Perhaps I had not fully understood what was really happening to me because so much information had been impossible to compute? I decided it must be reason number four because I had gone into information overload. All I really knew was I was in big trouble but some great people had told me they would make me better and give me my life back. All the detail in the overload pile was just a load of padding, which I did not need to know for this dance with Dolores. It is difficult to accept and fully understand exactly what is happening to you when you are so ill. When you are ill we really only need concentrate on getting better. Leave the detail to the professionals.

Getting your head around cancer is tough enough, but taking in all the information about a Chordoma and the effects of surgery and radiotherapy is very difficult, mainly because they are rare and there is not much data on which to develop an understanding or make decisions. A well-used statistic estimates they affect about one in a million people. Conventional thinking also claims they are very slow growing and I was told my Chordoma was very unusual in that it was huge and in a place where surgery would carry a lot of risks. We also discovered much later when preparing for the proton beam therapy in Florida, that Dolores was different again in that she showed herself to be particularly aggressive and fast growing.

Only one in seven million people are likely to develop a tumour like Dolores and I have to take on one that also breaks all the rules. Operating on the neck also carries its own set of risks. If particular nerves are cut or damaged during surgery I could have ended up unable to control my bladder or be paralysed. I hated the idea of being incontinent or having to cope with major changes that would substantially affect my quality of life. John and I are used to leading full and interesting lives. Sitting in a chair and involuntarily soiling myself was never going to be an option. I had always threatened to come back and haunt anybody who left me in a plastic armchair covered with a scratchy blanket.

My time in hospital was getting really interesting now and I was becoming fascinated by what was happening to me. I was grateful for my schooling where my teachers had encouraged me to take an interest in every experience and question everything I was told or read. I was also pleased how the jobs I had done had been about finding different ways to solve problems and look for new ways to help people learn. All my experiences had helped me develop the ability to look at things differently and not just look for the obvious. I am an unconventional thinker, which helps me see the positive side of life. I was not going to be miserable or to act a victim. I was delighted those handpicked teachers had used unconventional methods to teach me and even though some people I had worked with did sometimes think my ideas a little odd, it was now clear that all this time I had been preparing to deal with my current horrible situation. All I had been doing all that time was getting ready for my dance with Dolores.

I was woken from my deep sleep really early by a nurse who would help me prepare for my big day. It was still not bright outside. The first job was to wash me. Two nurses came in with a bowl of water. I said I could do it myself but they told me they had to do it. I was pleased because it meant I still did not have to look at Peggy. I had never been washed by someone else except my mother. I was allowed to wash my dangly bits myself, which was a relief for someone so modest.

I put on a clean surgical robe. After I was washed I sat in the armchair and my bed was changed. I was not allowed anything to eat. The eviction of Dolores would be done in two stages. Today was stage one. Today she would be attacked from the back. Mr Choi and his team would take Dolores by surprise by attacking her unawares through the back of my neck.

A little later Dr Katharine Hunt came to see me. Katharine is the clinical lead for resuscitation and the use of tracheostomy and so will keep me alive. Working with the anaesthetists my life is in her hands and I could not have wished for a friendlier, professional and more supportive person.

Mr Choi, Ernest and Michelle came to see me to tell me everything was in place. There were a couple of more routine procedures that would be done first so they could concentrate on me. I was wheeled down to the operating theatres at 11.20am. A host of people fussed around me. Mr Choi came in to see me. Katharine held my hand. I felt strangely comfortable, secure and relaxed. My blood pressure was taken. I was told I would go off to sleep quite soon. Woo, woo, gone.

While I was having my operation, Shimon Peres the ex-President and ex-Prime Minister of Israel died from a stroke. As the Minister for Defence he approved the raid on Entebbe Airport in Uganda in 1976 when 248 passengers were rescued from two terrorists by Israeli commanders. It was now Mr Choi's first opportunity to rescue me from Dolores.

Ernest rang John to tell him the operation had gone better than expected but I would not be woken up for another twelve or fourteen hours. People have often asked me what the operations were like. I have no idea. I was asleep, which is just as well. I was moved to intensive care. I was not woken up until 12.30pm the next day. John and Lisa came to see me. I was surprised visitors were allowed into the intensive care unit. Was this hygienic? I felt fine; John and Lisa were shocked by how well I looked. Ernest came and told me the operation lasted nine hours and I had lost three litres of blood. But where did all the blood go and who had actually cleaned it up? But it had all been a huge success.

John and Lisa told me they had just seen a lovely jacket in a local shop which Lisa was thinking of buying Kevin. 'Don't buy it for him, buy it for me,' I blurted out. 'He has loads of jackets.'

A lovely Dutch nurse was monitoring me by observing various machines to which I was attached. I asked him why he had come to London. He explained that to get the best training and plaudits on a CV it was essential to attend a great teaching hospital either in the States or the UK, because this is where the best research in the world is done. He felt privileged to be working at the National Hospital for Neurology and Neurological Surgery. I knew I was privileged to be a patient there.

By 2.00pm I was deemed well enough to move to the high dependency unit. I did not sleep well. I did not sleep the second night either. The ward was noisy. Patients needed a lot of nursing. I had my blood pressure taken so often I got confused about the time of day. The nurses moved me around in the bed to keep me comfortable. They were impressed I could already pull myself up in the bed using my elbows and pushing on my legs.

On Saturday evening I was moved from the HDU to Victor Horsley, which is one of the regular nursing wards. The nurse in charge was not happy about my arrival because he was understaffed and they did not have a bed space for me. I was put in the surgical preparation area next to the main ward. I had been here over two weeks ago when I came in to have one of my main arteries isolated. I did not mind, it was quiet and as it turned out I stayed there for the week.

My only real worry at the time was the kitchen staff might not realise I was in this area tucked behind my blue curtains. But my dinner did turn up and it was lovely. I would have hated to miss my meals. I read for a bit and the nurses made sure I had enough pain killers and they regularly took my blood pressure. I fell asleep before lights out and slept like a baby.

By Monday I was able to wash myself. The nurses brought me a bowl, wash cloths and a towel. I was back in pyjamas and the surgical gown was history for a few days. The nurses helped me walk and I sat in a chair. I went off for an MRI in a wheelchair. I was doing everything I could to get my strength back so the second operation would go ahead as planned. On Tuesday I shaved and had a shower below the neck. I was not allowed to get my neck wet. I was using a proper toilet and I felt human and civilised again.

Mr Choi said I had healed well. He had also decided to do the second operation by going through the front and not through the side of my neck. This meant he would have to use highly developed precision tools to cut and break open my jaw. I was filled with horror. It all seemed so barbaric and medieval. But I was assured that surgically this would be the most effective way of performing the procedure even though the healing time would take longer.

During the few days between my two big operations, I had a stream of visitors. John came every day to keep me company and sometimes friends would take him out for coffee to Lamb's Conduit Street. Not being in the main ward proved to be quite good because my friends and I were not disturbed and we did not have to worry about disturbing other people.

My second big day arrived just a week after my last operation. The operation planned for today was huge. It would be scary, complicated and last for hours. I was due to have several operations where the team would remove the rest of the tumour, fit titanium rods to my skull and the back of my neck and fit carbon fibre around my throat. I would have a tracheotomy fitted so I would be able to breathe during recovery. Fitting the tracheotomy would also give my throat, mouth and nose the freedom to heal over the next few weeks.

I wondered if Mr Choi ever thought about what he was letting himself in for. Did he sleep well before such a big event? Did he just get up like it was just another day and have a healthy breakfast? Do surgeons eat like us or do they have different feeding patterns? What strategies do they use to cope with the huge pressures they must be under and the gory sights they must witness?

I decided the operations were only difficult for me. They were of course complicated and complex but Mr Choi knows what he is doing and he is surrounded by a team of highly trained professionals who carry out their roles expertly. Mr Choi knows what he is doing and is able to direct and manage what needs to be done.

There are people among us who are that bit more special; perhaps they have been touched by God.

I was woken at six o'clock so I could get ready. The surgical preparation staff were in for a busy morning. Wednesday always seemed busy at the National. But I was surprised how quickly all the beds around me filled up. Some patients would only be in for the day. Others would stay. I had washed and I put on the horrible white surgical stockings. I could not eat or drink of course. Mr Choi and his team came to see me. They told me I was in good hands. I did not want to hear the risks. I signed the consent papers.

I was left on my own for a couple of hours but there was a lot to occupy me as I lay listening to the noises of the surgical preparation ward. Other patients were arriving and being prepared for their operations. I could hear wives discussing the up and coming operations or procedures with their husbands, but I only got snatches of what they were saying because their conversations were often interrupted by the arrival of visiting surgeons, nurses and anaesthetists or perhaps they just remembered where they were and lowered their voices so as not to be heard. I failed to piece together all the bits of conversations I could barely hear into sensible bits of information, so I gave up and started to think about where I was.

My thoughts turned to dying. I had learned about the risks of surgery and I knew how dangerous Dolores had become and I felt the odds of surviving surgery were stacked against me. This feeling of sorrow was new and unfamiliar to me because I had led a mainly charmed and unbroken life. My gods had been kind to me. I did not mind the sorrow and I discovered I was not scared of dying. Until you are actually faced with the prospect of death you never really know if you will be scared to die. I began to feel sorry for people who had been killed suddenly in accidents because they had never actually explored how they would feel about dying. They had not been given the chance to develop a relationship with death. I was lying in my bed able to make peace with myself. Death itself was not scary, leaving people behind and ending the experience of life was sad and this brought the sorrow.

I was not scared to die but I would be sorry not to continue living. I was feeling melancholy because I might not see the kids grow up or have fun spending my pensions. I wanted to survive the operation of course, but if I had to die I was pleased it would be in the autumn. It seemed beautifully poetic to die when the leaves were at their most glorious but dying and falling from the trees. I took comfort from my lonely moments of peaceful sorrow and melancholy. I fell into a deep sleep.

At 11 o'clock Mr Choi and Ernest came to see me. They had troubling news. They might have to postpone the operation because my titanium rods could not be sterilised in time for the operation. The sterilisation equipment at UCLH on the Euston Road had broken down. They promised to keep me posted. A little later Mr Choi came to tell me that London Bridge hospital had agreed to sterilise them. This was great news, not just for me but for the whole team and everybody involved because of all the planning that had taken place to get to this point. Getting ready for this operation had been like organising a military campaign.

I went to the operating theatre at two o'clock; a bit later than planned. I knew the process well. Lots of lovely talk, reassurance and kind people and then woo, woo, gone.

The operation lasted over nine hours this time and again I lost three litres of blood, which seemed such a lot. Ernest rang John well after 11 o'clock to tell him the operation had been a huge success. I found out much later that John had had a bad day. He knew this surgery was enormous and involved a number of tricky procedures and he had lived through the trauma and worry of the other operation. Siobhan went to the flat to keep him company, but when she arrived Siobhan was surprised to see John unusually dishevelled. John is always well turned out and takes a pride in his appearance, but on this occasion he was worried and a bit fed up. He surprised Siobhan by not having shaved or washed his hair and was dressed in a sloppy tracksuit. Siobhan had never expected John not to be on top form.

The day also tired him because friends kept ringing to see if there was any news and Ernest did not ring until just before midnight. By the time he dragged himself to bed John was completely drained emotionally and physically wrecked. When a person is ill it is often worse for the people close to the patient who have to be strong and carry on as normal as possible. John was marvellous during my stay in hospital, even when his world was completely torn inside out he visited me every day and coped with all our broken routines.

The strangest thing about the operations is they must be the biggest things that happened to me and yet I know hardly anything about them or what happened. Perhaps I can buy the video. I was asleep of course, which is just as well because I do not believe I could write about or do justice to these gory, horrendous but marvellous moments.

5. S.L.O.G

'When life brings you mountains, you don't waste your time asking why; you spend your time climbing over them.'

A J Darkholme

After the surgery I was not consciously aware of anything for four days. I was totally at the mercy of the medications that had taken over my brain. I did not know how I felt or what I was thinking. The world I was now experiencing was like nothing I had known before.

Instinctively I knew things were wrong but I did not know what was wrong. I could not work out how to communicate with John or the medical staff. I was desperate to tell let them know how awful things were but I was not sure if they were even there and I did not know how to reach them. I just wanted what was happening to me to stop. I could not experience normal human emotions like happiness or fear. I was just aware of confusion, which was made worse because it could not be explained. I knew I was not in control of my brain, but I did not know what I needed to do to take control of what I was thinking. I was drowning in my own confusion. Nothing made sense.

The confusion was so bad I did not know when I was awake or asleep. My head was all over the place. I was not sure which ward I was in or what day of the week it was. It could have been day or night. I was a sick person. I had a huge headache and people were not making sense.

When I slept it got worse. Nightmares would take over and disorientate me even more.

I remember how the nurses made me comfortable after my first day on the intensive care unit. I felt so warm and secure I fell asleep. But the drugs were not going to let me enjoy the night. The first nightmare began to run around the inside of my skull.

I was lying in my coffin ready for my funeral and I could hear my friends laughing and telling stories about me. Behind a curtain I could see loads of booze that friends were drinking to toast me on my way. From where I was I could not see my friends. I hoped they had all dressed up for the occasion. A number of people from the press had turned up because my cancer had been so rare. I heard John telling Neil not to let them in. John did not want the gentlemen of the press to see me for fear they might find out what he and Mr Choi were planning. I tried to shout but my body was dead. Mr Choi and John had killed my body but they could not kill my soul.

To stop people finding out what they had done, Mr Choi had a plan. It was tricky and I heard him tell John it might not work. John decided it was worth the risk. Mr Choi planned to take my soul and put it in a duck. I would be sent to a regeneration project in Stafford where I would live out my days on a pond. Every day a Labrador would come and chase me. I was so frustrated. I would not be able to tell anybody who I really was. I would be trapped inside a duck. I was witnessing my own funeral and to top it all, the buffet was not up to the standard I would have liked.

From my coffin I could hear people whispering and plotting. I heard John and Mr Choi talking to a nurse. The nurse came to me and pulled back the curtains. I looked past her and I could see the silhouettes of John and Mr Choi against the curtains. They are leaning in to hear what is happening. The nurse says she has something to help me rest. She rubbed my arm to prepare me for the injection. I am helpless. I cannot do anything to stop her or defend myself. One sharp prick and the evil deed was done. I was ready to have my soul taken out of my dead body.

When I woke three nurses were changing my sweaty bed to make me comfortable. I was given pain killers and something to help me sleep. This was to be the first of four terrifying and confusing nightmares

At this stage, I did not even realise I was peeing through a catheter or being fed through a drip attached to a cannula sticking out of my arm. I had stitches in my chin, tongue and throat, my lungs were being supplied with oxygen through a hole in my neck with the help of a tracheotomy, my neck was being supported by a neck brace called a Miami J Collar, because the titanium rods in the back of my neck and the carbon fibre in my throat were not yet ready to support my fragile old spine and on top of this I had not noticed the 'cricket pads' I was wearing, which kept squeezing my legs to help make sure my blood was circulating properly.

Then there were the wounds in the back of my neck, my chin, tongue and throat, which would eventually turn into scars that would become my trophies. I also found out later when I began to return to normal that I could not talk, walk or swallow. But before my recovery could fully begin, I was to have more scary dreams causing three more confusing and unsettling nights.

These nights proved to be the worst four nights of my adult life. I have always had bad dreams and as a kid awful nightmares. These night terrors had put the fear of God into my parents and sister. I often woke up at least three times a week screaming. I was often found in the bathroom having a terrible time after being chased into a burning cement mixer by a group of ugly, skinny and poorly dressed goblins.

The main characters in my second dream were our two friends Robert and Mark, who we have known for more than twenty five years. We met Robert when he was a member of the club we helped run on Bond Street and when he was still working as a trader in the City. We used to see each other every weekend and go on annual holidays together. During one trip to Paris we were on top of the Arc de Triomphe in the days when people still had cameras instead of mobile phones. Sharing the views with us was a Japanese couple. The lady asked Robert if he would take a photograph for her of her and her husband. Robert was pleased to oblige and stepped back and took a photograph with his own camera. John, Mark and I could not stop laughing and the developed photograph showed two shocked tourists from Japan.

In this dream Robert and Mark were using my stay in hospital as an excuse to steal drugs.

They had got friendly with a nurse who they had persuaded to steal the drugs for them. The nurse was a bit plain and had fallen for Mark's compliments. She was flattered by his attention. They were paying her peanuts for the drugs, which they were selling on the streets of Edinburgh. When they left me they went straight to King's Cross station to catch a train to Scotland where they were making a fortune.

I was in a pickle. Should I do the right and legal thing and report them to the police. This was causing me terrible anxiety. A blue light was flashing in the street below. The police had arrived and I could hear Robert and Mark talking in hush tones. They were blaming each other. Mark said to Robert he must have phoned the police. Robert told Mark not to be so stupid. I heard the nurse crying. I racked my brains to try and remember if I had phoned the police. How could I, I did not even have a phone, but the guilt made me feel sick. Robert came in and sat by my bed.

'Hello Bim, how are you?' Robert often calls me Bim. I asked what the police were doing. He said what police? Mark was shouting at the nurse to shut up. The police car drove off. We were all in the clear. All, what did I mean all; I was innocent for goodness sake? I was getting more and more confused and I was covered in sweat.

The nurse and Mark came in to see Robert. I told them I knew what they were doing. I told them I would shop them if they did not stop themselves. The nurse pleaded with me. She was in such a mess. She said she could not afford to lose her job because she had a little boy to look after. I had cut off their supplier so Mark and Robert had no choice but to stop. Robert broke down and confessed he was relieved. A policeman violently pulled back the curtain.

'Okay you're under arrest - hit the floor punks,' he ordered.

I woke up shaking. I was finding it impossible to distinguish between reality and fantasy. I was losing days. The dreams I was having were horrible and not doing me any good at all. I was terribly confused and I was sweating all the time. The heat was unreal. I was burning up. When John and Lisa came to visit me I had just been moved to the HDU. They could not believe what I was doing. The nurses had given me a bowl of iced water. I was putting lumps of ice on my head until it melted. To me this was heaven. I was of course very wet. The water was running down my face and neck.

Lisa was shocked at the sight of my hands. They were completely white and looked like they belonged to a corpse. This must have been because of the blood I lost and it took two weeks for them to return to normal.

I could not talk because of the tracheotomy in my windpipe. The nurses had given me some paper and a pen, which I used to write down answers to questions but I did not really have a clue what I was writing down or where I was. I wrote John an instruction and asked him to go and look behind a curtain on the other side of the ward because I was convinced there had been fighting last night and I was sure someone had been murdered. I could still hear the policemen and nurses talking from behind the curtain every time I looked over to where I thought the murder had taken place. But of course I had been in ITU last night not here in the HDU. Humour the poor little patient. John and Lisa decided the paper was not such a good idea because it was awkward and not a firm surface on which to write. My writing was awful and difficult to read and so they went out in search for a whiteboard and felt tip pens. I think they were probably relieved to get away from me for a while. They returned with the whiteboard and pens which I would use over the next couple of weeks to communicate with staff and visitors.

Lisa and John left. The nurses washed me again. They changed the sheets and put me in a new surgical gown. They made me comfortable by propping me up on pillows. I felt relaxed at last. It was Saturday night. I thought about all my Saturday nights at dinner parties and nightclubs. Saturdays were for play, not bad dreams, bed baths and bed pans.

The nurses gave me my medicines through the cannula and I drifted off to have my third nightmare. I was in a backstreet about to enter an illegal medical practise run by a ruthless mother and daughter. The mother was from New Delhi. She had had a medical training but had been struck off for malpractice and corruption back in India. She had come to London and set up an illegal clinic in a poorly lit alley in Soho. She charged a fortune for her services and did not much care about any rules and regulations. The people who went to her were desperate. She performed abortions on women and treated sexually transmitted diseases for people who wanted to keep things quiet or who had something to hide and so could not be treated by legitimate doctors. Her twilight services were popular and she and her daughter were making a fortune.

I had a sexually transmitted disease which was getting hard to treat. I was going blind and was finding it difficult to walk because my legs were swollen and ulcerated. I entered her treatment rooms through a candy shop, which was an excellent cover because it looked so innocent and colourful. A lovely middle aged woman managed the shop.

'Good afternoon,' I said. 'I don't like sweets; they give me the burps,' I told her. This was the code people used to get into the clinic. Her expression changed. She realised I was there for something more than sweets. She pulled back a curtain and sent me through to the hidden clinic.

The reception looked entirely respectable. It was clean, bright and even boasted a huge rubber plant. A tall beautiful woman greeted me. She took me to the basement and told me her mother would be with me soon. The poorly lit room was stuffy, hot and filthy. The bed linen was soiled and the floor was sticky. A steel table next to the bed was greasy and covered in old medicines. Blood stained and soiled bandages lay on the floor. The mother came to see me. She made me swallow a vile tasting concoction. She took great pleasure in changing my dressings because she hurt me. She was vile and cruel. To say she was ugly would be an understatement. She had warts all over her face. Her nose was huge and hooked. Her bony fingers tormented my sore body. I pleaded with her to stop what she was doing.

'You're not here to be cured. You're here to be punished. How do you think you got your disease, singing hymns in church?' she growled.

A patient lying in the bed next to me told me the only way out was up the fireman's pole in the corner of the room. He told me the police would not get her because she had a private aeroplane fuelled up and waiting on the tarmac if she needed to escape quickly.

I waited until it was quiet and started to climb the pole. It was hard work but I did it. I found myself in the store room of the sweet shop. I hopped through the shop and out into the street.

I woke to find the nurses settling me down again.

By Sunday my life started to return to normal and it was beginning to make more sense when John and Siobhan came to visit me. John and Siobhan answered my questions, which I had written down before they arrived. I used the questions to begin to piece together where I was and what had happened to me. They told me how long I had been out of my skull and they could not help but laugh. John told me I had had my second operation and had not made any sense for the last three days. He made me shudder when he told me about the ice cubes. He had stopped people from visiting me and we agreed not to let people come for a few more days.

The last scary dream was much more fanciful and Disneyesque. I was living in a magical forest. The trees and other plants thickly covered the forest floor and they were not just green. They were all vivid colours. Some were purple with yellow flowers; others were blue with green and orange flowers. This magical forest had rivers and waterfalls, which fell over vast craggy cliffs. The forest was also inhabited by all sorts of exotic animals. It was very friendly and all the creatures seemed to be getting on well. There was no shortage of food and everything tasted good. I was not sure if I was on the set of Avatar or in a Disney cartoon from the 1940s.

We were all lying around enjoying the fruits of the forest when the peace was disturbed by the arrival of a huge character richly dressed in dark browns and greens. His cloak was decorated in leaves made from gold thread. His hair resembled the branches of a tree. His arrival was announced by a fanfare of trumpets. All the creatures stood up and their mood changed. They started muttering to each other. They began to look nervous. The monster's announcement boomed through the forest.

'The time has come for you to give thanks to your bountiful god. If you want this wonderful life to continue you will need to take part in the games for the entertainment of your benefactor. If he is pleased with the games he will allow you to continue living here. Choose your competitors for the flying race wisely and remember only half of those picked will survive. May the best oddballs win and god rest the souls of those who do not,' and with this he simply faded away and was gone.

Against my wishes I was chosen to take part. I had no choice because I was the newest creature to come and live in the forest. I was also human and regarded as ugly. I was not magical or colourful and my clothes were plain and boring, so if I died it would not matter. I was given a chariot made out of a pod from a local tree. It was painted in bright colours and pulled by two bad tempered flying horses. I climbed aboard the chariot and put on my gold helmet. Without any starting gun or whistle the chariot raced off as soon as I took hold of the reigns. My eleven competitors chased after me. We flew up the side of cliffs and swooped down into deep valleys. The horses were quick but I could not really control them. I quickly discovered the other competitors were not racing each other.

They were hell bent on destroying me. Six had to die and I was to be the first. One of the bigger chariots was gaining on me. I saw a small bridge ahead of me I pulled the reigns and the horses took me low and I flew under the bridge. The bigger fellow followed me and crashed into the granite walls. I saw him thrown onto the riverbank. One down. I swooped up at ninety degrees and two other chariots flew to chase me but they did not see each other, crashed and disappeared into the richly coloured forest below. Three down. I was getting confident. Perhaps I was a bit too confident. I was looking behind me when I crashed into a tree. The chariot flew off and left me battered and broken hanging in its bows. My race was over.

I woke in a massive gothic hospital that stood on a windy and rocky cliff. With huge turrets and vast stained glass windows it dominated the pine covered landscape. The nurse who attended me was green and had reptilian features. She told me I would die so they could all now go back to living the good life. She turned away from me and I saw the hypodermic needle she had raised to the light. As she squeezed out the air, little drops of her poison escaped as a small fountain. She turned, grinned menacingly and with huge delight stuck the needle in the top of my arm. I thrashed around on the bed, but the gothic windows in the huge ward where I was laying began to spin and I felt sick. The hammer beam ceiling came down and hit me hard in the face; I heard my nose crack and my world went black.

In the early hours of Monday morning I woke screaming and fighting. My nurses were holding me down so I would not disconnect myself from the equipment being used to keep me safe. I would not be consoled. I cannot remember clearly what happened, but I apologise sincerely to the nurses who helped me that terrible night. They made me comfortable and I fell into a quieter and more relaxed sleep.

I woke to a bright sunny autumn morning. The physiotherapists helped me get up and they sat me in the chair next to my bed. My cricket pads were removed and replaced by a pair of those horrible white surgical stockings, which I hated. I was feeling much better and Mr Choi thought me strong enough to have an MRI scan, which in itself was a challenge because I had to be transported to the imaging unit with all the equipment being used to help me breathe and monitor how well I was recovering piled up on the bed around me. I decided I would have made a great rag and bone man. Getting on the table for the MRI could have been a scene from a Carry On film. Several medical staff held all my attachments while others put me on a paddle board so I could be slipped sideways onto the table. Getting off the table after the MRI scan and back onto my bed was just as silly and I enjoyed the sense of the ridiculous.

The activities of the day must have tired me because during my last night on the HDU, I slept peacefully without any bad dreams to disturb me. The following day I was moved to the Victor Horsley ward, where over the next three weeks I would improve my stamina, learn to walk, talk and swallow again and over time rid myself of everything that was attached or inserted in me so I could go home to convalesce.

Nothing can prepare you for a stay in hospital. It is nothing like anything I had ever done. I had slept in dormitories on school holidays years ago, but this was so different to anything I had experienced before. I could only learn how to live and behave on a ward by learning on the job. I quickly got used to how the day was organised. We woke early, washed and the beds were changed. Medicines were administered and doctors made their rounds. I soon fell into the ward's rhythms and I could see why people might become institutionalised. Life on the ward was easy, cosy, well ordered and stress free. Everything was done for me and I quickly began to enjoy my stay on Victor Horsley. I am reluctant to admit it but I also loved being the centre of attention. Friends came to visit me and they genuinely wanted to know how

I was. They sat with me and we talked and laughed. Who would not like to be looked after by caring professionals and visited by friends all the time? Friends also brought me presents. I was to discover in the future how much I would miss all this attention as my life gradually returned to normal. Add to this the time to read books, newspapers and watch films on John's iPad and I concluded a spell in hospital was more than okay.

Even though the bad dreams had stopped, I was still scared about going to sleep for the next few nights and I also had something new to contend with and this was in the daytime, when I was wide awake. A voice would for no reason suddenly shout vile things about God, Jesus and the Virgin Mary behind my right ear. This violent noise would rush past my head and disappear into the future. The words were so strong they almost took on a physical form. I would be reading in my bed or sitting in the chair and this vile little blasphemer would scream at me and then scarily disappear. The ward might even be noisy but this did not seem to worry my nasty little demon. It would arrive in a whisper, which turned into a shout and then streak away into a whisper again. Whoosh it would be here and gone in seconds.

It was such a bloody coward and I could never catch it. I sat and lived in fear of this demon's arrival, but it never came when I was waiting for it. It only turned up when I was unaware and not expecting a visit. I was scared of these visits and hated what was shouted at me. By the following Friday I became aware my little disgusting demon had left. I was not being shouted at anymore. Perhaps it had given up and knew I would not be upset about its views of God, Jesus and the Virgin Mary. To my great relief their reputations remained intact.

My pest did visit once more on the Sunday just to tell me:

'James Holyfield is a wankerrrrrr,' and whoosh it was gone.

So I had had the second big operation on Tuesday October 5th after which I lost five days being moved from the ITCU and HDU, where I passed the time having scary dreams, hallucinations and being shouted at by a vile little foul mouthed pest. I was now to spend the next three weeks setting myself goals before I would go home just four weeks after having my second serious operation. My recovery was marked by a series of events that would help me get well enough to leave hospital.

I loved my time on Victor Horsley ward. I slept like a log on the Tuesday night I first arrived and for most of the following nights. I had a bed right in front of the nurse's station and so I felt safe. It was a privilege to be looked after by such a talented and dedicated group of people. The only thing I missed was the meals. I was now getting my sustenance through a drip attached to a cannula in my arm. I had enjoyed the food in the National before my second operation. Meal times were now a bit of an ordeal for me. If anybody ever needed to punish me I could not think of a better way to do this than to deprive me of food. I love food. Always have. When my mum wanted to punish me she would send me to bed. I just went to sleep. I have always loved to sleep as well. Or perhaps I just have the knack of making the best of awful situations. I was in hospital but I had to recover from those serious and invasive operations. I decided to make the most of it and enjoy the experience; to witness the comings and goings on the ward and all the little dramas.

My first Wednesday on the ward was my best day yet. My nurse Dino asked if I wanted to wash myself. He brought me a bowl of warm soapy water, some washcloths and two towels. He closed the curtains and I got myself ready.

Washing yourself when just sitting in a chair was not as straightforward as it might seem. I was attached to a drip that fed and hydrated me and a catheter that took what went in away. One tube puts it in and another throws it out. Later experiences of washing myself were even more challenging because walking around the bed can be hazardous when attached to a catheter and I was warned not to stretch the drip.

Over time I got used to the manoeuvres necessary to keep myself clean, but I never got used to the catheter, which I hated. I hated the fact it hung on the side of the bed in full view of visitors. I would hang a blanket over it, but a bag company was missing an opportunity to make a fortune producing designer bags in which to slip catheters. Imagine them in different colours and materials. You might even have them monogrammed or personalised in some way. I always hated it when a nurse came to empty it. They told me it was important because they had to measure the volume of liquid. This kind of business and information had always been private in my family. Yuk. When I finished washing myself, I kept one towel back, which I would use to put over the back of the chair. This would make it more comfortable because the plastic chairs made me sweat.

After my wash I was sitting in my chair when Mr Choi and his team did their rounds. Mr Choi wanted to give me the results of that hilarious MRI scan I had had on Monday. Mr Choi confirmed the operations had been a success and he was impressed with my recovery so far. After all, it had only been eight days since the second huge operation. He told me most of the tumour had been successfully removed. Some cancer cells remained, but these would be managed and controlled with radiotherapy.

If I had not had the two operations I would have died, Dolores would have killed me. He had not been able to remove everything because of where the tumour had been. It would have been dangerous to cut away any more bone because I may have ended up paralysed. He had been concerned about my mobility. My spine had been weakened because large amounts of bone had been removed, which is why lots of construction had been required using titanium rods for the back of my neck and carbon fibre for my throat. He explained the swelling in my throat and mouth and around my neck was still of some concern. He congratulated me on how well I had recovered so far, in fact he said he was surprised at my progress because the tumour had been huge and very rare.

The tumour had been the size of a clenched fist or a small cauliflower. Some people might not have even survived such intensive, invasive and brutal surgery, where each operation had lasted nine hours and each time I lost three litres of blood. He put this down to the fact I was physically fit, slim and mentally positive. All the time spent at the gym over the last three years had all been worthwhile and I was grateful for the way I had been taught to look on the bright side.

After all this positive news, he advised me to be patient and told me to be realistic about my recovery time. At this stage he could not tell me when the stitches would be taken out or when the tracheotomy would be removed. He did not know when I would be able to speak or swallow again. He estimated I would need six to eight weeks recovery time. I would need to keep the neck brace on for at least six more weeks, which for me was the most depressing bit. As it turned out I was to wear it a lot longer than six weeks. The neck brace was tough to wear and get used to. It was made from an extremely hard plastic and it was lined with dark blue pads which were removed for washing. It came in two halves and it was fixed in place tight under my chin by joining the two halves using Velcro tapes. I wore it all the time; twenty four hours a day and it was only removed so the pads could be changed, when I had to lay flat on my bed and carefully hold my neck.

Mr Choi told me I could help the healing process by working to improve my mobility. He asked me to exercise and work with the physiotherapists by walking. He told me it would be good to set myself goals where I should aim to go to the toilet on my own and take showers. He was confident I would return to a normal life. I would have my life back. But for the time being there were still difficult times ahead, where the body would need to accept the rods and carbon fibre and I would have to learn to walk, speak and swallow again. It would take time and I was in no position to argue with him, so I just sat and listened.

After he and his team left, Michelle came back to see me. We went through what Mr Choi had told me and Michelle said they were all really pleased with what had happened. She confirmed the severity of the operations and the amazing outcomes and explained I was doing much better than anyone had expected, hoped for or anticipated. She told me I would see improvements each day. I wrote questions on the whiteboard and Michelle answered them for me.

I had a couple of hours to mull over what I had been told before Emma, my physiotherapist arrived to see me for the first time. During this time I went over what Mr Choi had said about me needing six to eight weeks to recover. I thought this was far too long and I set out to prove him wrong. I would recover quicker by working hard and setting myself goals. Emma and I went over how I felt and I explained what I was feeling on the whiteboard and she thought I ought to try walking. A nurse came to detach me from my drip. I was a bit anxious but did it. I walked the length of the ward with her encouragement and the help of a walker with two wheels. The one bit I hated was having to hang my catheter on the walker; where is my designer, monogrammed catheter bag? Wow, should I put my name down for next year's marathon? Has anyone run the marathon with a catheter? I did not even think I would be sitting up in bed by now.

I got back in bed and a nurse attached me to the drip again. With my movement restricted by the drip I was back in my own private prison, tethered to the bed. I saw the drip as my personal ball and chain.

It was a good day for visitors. John and Siobhan came at two o'clock. John was amazed how much I had done that morning. He suggested I have my father's old walking stick and agreed to bring it in the next day.

Howard came in at five on his way to the theatre. Howard loves the theatre and he even writes reviews about operas he sees. Howard is an inspiration. Nothing deters him and he just eats up life.

A nurse started visiting me every second day to ask how I was getting on. He told me sleep was essential to help the healing process. He wanted me to stay positive so the medical staff would be able to work with me to reduce my dependency on oxygen, remove my stitches and metal staples, remove the tracheotomy, lose the neck brace and get me talking and swallowing again. I was going to prove to Mr Choi I would not be in hospital for six to eight weeks.

Using the whiteboard, we agreed a list of goals, where I would learn to walk better so I would improve my mobility and grow stronger, use the toilet, take showers, aim to attend the annual Christmas party planned for early December and get back to the gym in the future. I wrote the goals down in my notebook and even added a few of my own.

I did not make the party and I did not return to the gym, but the goals kept me going.

Nurses were always asking me if I needed a bed pan and they were now worrying about my bowel movements. I was weeing buckets, but the other department had closed down. I hated this obsession with my poo. One evening I got a pain in my stomach and asked for a bed pan. It was so bloody awkward. Sitting on a bedpan wearing a neck brace following major surgery on my neck was nearly impossible. Then it started. The noises were unreal. I could do nothing about them and I wanted to hide under the bed. The nurse came in to help. I apologised for the mess as I lifted myself off the bloody thing.

'It's clean James,' she told me. 'You've delivered nothing but wind. I think you'd better have a laxative.' I had only spent the time farting, which I could not believe. We had a very pleasant and informative discussion about laxatives and I told her when I had used them in the past they had upset my system. I was a bit scared to take them. The nurse assured me they were different these days and said they would only loosen my stools, so I took them. Nothing happened.

I loved lunch times, not because I ate anything but at one o'clock the staff turned off all the lights and we had an hour's nap. I looked forward to this ritual every day. It was so peaceful and everybody was engaged in the same activity. We were not allowed visitors and all radios and televisions were turned off. Peace. I always fell asleep for the whole hour. The whole daily experience was absolute bliss.

I was getting a lovely stream of visitors now so Dr Stewart had been right about all the love that would come back to me. From my bed or my chair I had a good view of the door leading into the ward. This meant I could see my visitors before they saw me. I enjoyed this enormously because my visitors always walked in apprehensively. I supposed they were a bit concerned about what they were going to find lying in the bed. Would I be vile to look at? Would I be bandaged or covered in scabs? Did they expect to see a big bloated head lying on the pillow covered in stitches and metal clips? Would I have loads of tubes hanging out of my nose? I called this the big blue head moment.

I would lie in bed or sit looking down the ward to the door waiting to see who was coming. I used to love to see how for the first time my family and friends would gingerly walk in. Mark was the best when he came to see me on the Wednesday because he looked particularly worried.

'Actually you don't look too bad as it 'appens. Well I mean, what you've been through and all,' Mark always knows how to make you feel good. He dispatches his compliments with huge caution.

When Mark and Robert first walked in I experienced a moment of confusion as I wondered how they had escaped police custody. They were not wearing handcuffs and there were no police to be seen. For a second I was convinced they had been locked up. The morphine was still playing with my brain and occasionally I still found it difficult to distinguish real life from those horrible dreams and hallucinations. I think they felt a bit insulted when I told them about their antics in Edinburgh. They did not laugh.

I was also getting loads of get well cards and their number quickly doubled. Even though I knew I was showing off I displayed the cards above my bed and I was very protective of them. Even though I knew this was shallow of me I thought they demonstrated to other people how popular I was. But on the other hand strangers probably just assumed I had been in the National for months. After a while I took them down and kept them in a discreet pile by the bed next to the books and magazines.

Thursday marked my thirteenth week anniversary since the

biopsy. I knew I was on strong pain killers because of the operations, but to not have the pain I had experienced over the last sixteen months, especially during late July and August was worth all the hassle I had been through. I was going to have aches as my skull and neck grew to accept the titanium rods and carbon fibre, but this would not be anything like the pain Dolores inflicted on me as she danced in my neck. This Thursday also saw me having a series of X-rays, where I offered to stand, which seemed to surprise the radiologist and I did some more walking around the ward with Emma.

John came in with my walking stick at two o'clock followed by his cousins Mary and John. Mary was wearing a beautiful coat and looked stunning. I told her how lovely she looked and she said she had dressed up for me. I used the whiteboard to ask them if they had expected to see a big blue head and they said something like that and were surprised how quickly I had got to this stage in my recovery.

Conversations were of course a bit tortuous because I had to write down questions for my guests and my answers to their questions. Most times I did not have to finish a sentence because they often guessed where I was going and finished off my answers for me. I suggested John go out for a coffee with John and Mary and so they left to go to our favourite cafe on Lamb's Conduit Street. I got into bed and fell asleep for an hour before Pauline and Howard arrived. I told them all I had done. I was so proud.

On Friday Emma gave me a bigger challenge and suggested it was time to walk upstairs. But before this adventure the nurses had decided to remove my catheter and only two days after I had washed myself for the first time and only ten days since the second big operation. Things were looking good and just as Michelle had promised, I was seeing improvements every day. I was now beginning to believe I would manage to reduce my healing time. The nurses explained it was necessary to remove the catheter in order to avoid an infection. But I did not need convincing this was a good idea; I was delighted. I would now be able to use a proper toilet for most of the time. I would also be able to shower now but only from the chest down. I would not be able to wash my hair or get my dressings wet, so Lisa brought me in some dry shampoo, which I confess I never used. I had used it years ago and it was vile. Emma and I left the ward and walked round to the apples and pears. I walked up two flights. I used the handrail and left my father's stick at the bottom. Coming down was a bit trickier than going up. I had this sensation of falling.

After a recovery break back in bed, Emma and one of her colleagues returned with an exercise cycle. Emma had asked me earlier if I wanted to try it. I had visualised an upright cycle like those in gyms and thought I might have to do a spin class. To my relief it was a sit down affair. I got into the seat, put my feet in the pedals and peddled away. It was much more difficult than I expected and I tired really quickly. I got out of breath. Emma said I would use the cycle to build up my stamina and improve my breathing over the next few days. The cycle proved to be the toughest challenge yet and I was not looking forward to Monday when I would be tested again. I blamed my poor stamina on the tracheotomy. I got back in bed and a nurse came to tether me to my drip.

I had so much to write on the whiteboard when John, Meryl, Neil and Nichola came to visit. They kept telling me how well I was doing. They came with gifts including a posh hand cream from Nichola, playing cards and two books from Meryl. I was getting used to being spoiled and loved it.

I do not know if it was because I did too much on that Friday, but I could not fall asleep. I lay awake for hours listening to all the noises of the ward. It was a really difficult night for me. The nurse on duty gave me a sleeping pill, but for some reason it did not work. Hospital wards are never dark. Night lights are left on, which create relaxed and comforting atmospheres. I lay in the comfortable weak light thinking about what had happened to me. I could not believe I was still alive or how I had got this far so soon. I was counting my blessings and trying to put in order everything that had happened to me over the last months when I must have fallen asleep without realising it at about three o'clock.

It seems strange how Mr Sleep will eventually take over. But why was he late tonight, had he missed the last tube? Perhaps he was having a good time in a pub somewhere, when the publican had decided to have a lock-in.

I was not breathing through my mouth or nose because I was using the tracheotomy inserted in my windpipe. This simple piece of kit meant I was able to breath and therefore survive. I began to see my tracheotomy as a muscular no nonsense lifeguard called Guy Pike. Guy worked indoors during the winter at the local sports centre, but during the summer months he could be found strutting his stuff down on the beaches of Bournemouth. He was not the most handsome fella, but his quirky looks and athletic build made him popular with the ladies.

To help me breathe I was sometimes given an oxygen mask, which was held over the entrance to the tracheotomy but this did lead to a problem. The oxygen made my breathing easier but it came at a price because it dried out my breathing tubes and phlegm formed in my lungs. It was a shame that someone as fit looking as Guy Pike actually seemed to be an asthma sufferer. After a while I could hear the phlegm rattling in my chest. The problem was I could not shift it because I did not have the use of my throat or mouth and so I could not cough. My nurses were worried this problem might cause a lung infection, so they regularly cleared my airways of the offending phlegm.

The procedure they used was one of the worst things I had to endure. I dreaded and feared it. The whole procedure came with its own set of rituals. The nurse would put on surgical gloves and deliberately lay out all the equipment to be used. A three foot tube of thin malleable plastic was removed from its paper cover with great aplomb and then inserted into my airways through the hole in my tracheotomy. A pump was used to suck out the phlegm. As the sucking took place, my chest tightened and a feeling of panic overtook me because I could not breathe until the tube had finished its job and was removed. I imagined this was what it must be like to drown. To be deprived of air and the panic that goes with it must make drowning a horrible way to leave the planet. Sometimes a nurse would decide to repeat the procedure a second time just to make sure the offending phlegm was properly dealt with. After the long plastic tube was removed Guy Pike was taken out of my windpipe, washed and then put back. The whole procedure was truly vile, scary and horrible but the feeling of being able to breathe properly afterwards was lovely.

Weekends are strange times in hospital. Weekdays are full of activity with doctors, physiotherapists, swallow nurses, pharmacists, volunteers, porters, and all sorts of specialist nurses rushing in and out and around doing things, talking and filling in computer records. Patients are whisked off by porters for operations, medical procedures, X-rays and various scans. Administrators come on shift to assist the nursing staff. Even therapy dogs visit with their handlers to cheer up the patients. Witnessing the hive of activity can be exhausting.

Weekends are completely different. The ward slows down. Beds are still changed of course and patients are given their medicines and they still have their blood pressure and temperature taken on a regular basis. But it is more genteel and meal times seem less frantic. Weekends give you more time to relax and this is the best time to read, watch films, keep a diary, fall asleep and heal.

But this Saturday morning was particularly good because, without the catheter, I could for the first time use the toilet and the shower. After being released from the drip I took myself off to the bathroom. My nurse decided I was well enough to shower on my own. This was the first time I had been on my own in a private space for ages and I wanted to enjoy it. I took off my pyjamas and on cue my stomach rumbled. In the privacy of a proper toilet my body gave the laxatives permission to work. I thanked all the gods in heaven this had not happened in bed on a bedpan. I could not understand how the brown sludge which had dripped into me since my operation could change into such a bright horrible colour. I was totally shocked and nearly convinced that what I produced could only have been produced by an alien. When I returned to my bed my nurse asked me if I was okay as she tethered me back to my drip.

'I am yes. Thanks. But I went to the toilet and the colour was awful,' I replied. It was not a colour I would pick if buying a shirt.

'Don't worry about that; it'll be all the mix of drugs you are on. You had strong doses of morphine,' she told me. 'I should have probably warned you. Sorry.'

'Don't worry; I'm glad you've told me about what the drugs can do to me. I was embarrassed to mention it; so apologies from me too. I was in two minds whether to say something, but I thought you should know in case something was wrong,' I said.

I really enjoyed my shower. I could have sat down, but I decided to test my strength by standing. I had to shower below my neck and I could not get the neck brace wet, but the smell of shower gel, the feel of hot running water and my wet skin was better than swimming in the Mediterranean in August. When I dried myself I stood and looked at my body in the strange mirror made of plastic and what I thought must be aluminium foil. It did not reflect a true picture of my shape and it would not have been out of place in a hall of mirrors attraction on the end of Brighton Pier, but the mirror could not disguise the colour of my body which was a bit of a shock that caught me unawares. I looked like a cuttlefish bone you might buy a budgie for its cage. I could not have been whiter and my ribcage seemed enormous compared to the one I had looked at only two weeks ago. I breathed in and pushed it out further to see how thin I could make my legs look. I was turning into that alien.

When John came in to visit I asked him to bring me in some proper clothes that I could wear in the daytime. I was showering and things were getting back to the way I wanted and I only wanted to wear pyjamas in bed, not live in them.

Our friends Sue and John came to see me on Sunday. We have known these two special people for years. My John first spoke to Sue at a party where he pretended to read her palm and they became instant friends. Sue organised my fiftieth birthday party in the wine cellar on Regent's Street. We have been horse racing with them but we rarely see the races because we are far too busy eating good food and drinking. We have often staggered home after losing our betting money. They were the first visitors to ever visit in the morning. They came at eleven. Sue looked her usual glamorous self. I wrote on the whiteboard to tell them I was keeping notes and a diary of what was happening in case I ever decided to write a book about my experiences. Sue took my diary and wrote an entry for me to see after they left.

'Sue and John came today, they are rab,' I read later. What did she mean? It took me ages before I saw the letter r was actually the letter f. I should have read 'Sue and John came today, they are fab.' I learned later that when they left, Sue cried when they got to the lift because she had been shocked how thin I was and she was sure this would be the last time she would see me alive.

Mr Choi came to see me on the morning of the new working week and again he told me how pleased he was with my recovery, but I was a bit disappointed when he told me I would probably be connected to the drip for another four weeks. I wanted to be cut free from the last thing restricting my movement. If I wanted to go to the toilet or have a shower a nurse first had to unhook me from my brown protein sludge. I also knew I would not be allowed to leave hospital until the feeding drip was history. It also meant I had to use bottles in the night if I wanted a wee. It was too much trouble to ask a nurse to unhook me at three in the morning. But I refused to let this news upset me when I reminded myself I was on a mission to prove Mr Choi wrong and help Sue feel a bit better.

Over the next few days I worked hard to achieve a number of goals. I cycled for fifteen minutes on a gradient set at four. The stitches in my chin were removed. On Friday Emma took me for my first walk outside in Queen's Square. The weather was gorgeous. The leaves were turning gold and the air had a fresh bite to it.

But the really big milestone was being able to make Guy Pike redundant. On the morning of the next Wednesday Katharine and my swallow nurse came to see if I could be weaned off the tracheotomy. I was warned it might not work and should be prepared to be disappointed. I loved these two ladies who had so much faith in me. They were kind, encouraging but totally honest about what was achievable. Guy Pike was simply a short plastic tube that was inserted into my windpipe. This tube was held in place by what I called my manhole cover. The manhole cover covered the hole in my throat. Katharine removed the tracheotomy and covered the hole with a blue stopper. I was asked to breathe in through my nose and out through my mouth. We practiced a few times. Air was now passing over my voice box and so Katharine thought it might be time to see if I could make a noise. Again they warned me it might take time, perhaps even a few days and warned me not to be too disappointed. I made an 'arrrgggghhh' sound and an 'eeemmmm' sound. After thirty seconds I spoke. I was breathing properly and I was talking again. Katharine and my swallow nurse were delighted. Mr Choi was so pleased he decided that later in the afternoon he would put a camera up my nose and down my throat to see how well my throat was healing. It was amazing how quickly breathing felt normal again.

In the meantime John came in to see me after lunch. The nurses and admin staff had decided what I should do. I pretended to be asleep when John came in. I pretended to wake up and got into my chair. John began to ask questions and I gestured to him to pass me the white board. All the staff were observing us from the nurses station. I began to write out the answer to his question on the whiteboard, stopped and looked up.

'Oh bugger it. I don't need this anymore. You can take it home,' I said loudly as I passed him the redundant whiteboard. The staff laughed and clapped. John looked confused and shocked. For a second he thought I had talked through the hole in my neck. The penny did not drop straight away because he could not believe it. I had not given him any warning that Guy Pike was about to be paid off. In his excitement he could not stop talking about how pleased he was and he kept thanking the staff. We laughed about it for ages. John waited for me when I went off to see Mr Choi.

Looking back to the movie Sunset Boulevard I thought this was my Cecil B DeMille moment. Like Gloria Swanson I was ready for my close up Mr DeMille. Mr Choi sprayed the inside of my nose but the tube containing the camera still tickled me. The camera went up my nose and down my throat and the image was projected onto a computer screen. Mr Choi and members of his team seemed impressed. I was told the healing was excellent and the top stitches in my throat had already dissolved. The stitches in my lower throat were still there and the throat was still swollen as was my tongue. This was the moment I found out Mr Choi had cut my tongue in half, which was stitched and quite swollen. It was also numb and this was the reason why I had not been able to feel my lower front teeth which I had assumed were gone. I thought I had lost my teeth when my jaw was cut and opened up. But they were there and I had not lost any teeth after all. Hooray.

On a couple of occasions I had wanted to open my mouth and look in a mirror to see what was going on in my mouth, but I could not pluck up courage to do it because I did not know how I might react to seeing no teeth and a ravaged jaw.

After such an exciting day John went home delighted for me and a bit later Meryl came to visit me. I played the same trick on Meryl by pretending I could not talk. Meryl actually jumped when I spoke. Sleep came easily that night.

I was breathing normally and clearing my chest on my own. No more long tubes down the throat or that terrifying drowning feeling. But this was funny because if I got the cough right I could blow out the blue stopper from my manhole cover, which gave me great delight. I just loved seeing how far I could make it fly.

After the third weekend since my last operation the staples in the back of my head were taken out with the staple remover. I thought it was going to hurt and be horrible, but it was okay. On Tuesday the rest of the tracheotomy was removed and the hole in the front of my neck was covered with a huge clean dressing. With help from my swallow nurse I learned how to swallow again. I was drinking again. It was only water, but I was swallowing.

It was now nine days since I had been told I might have to stay on the drip feed for four more weeks but all the progress I had made during this time meant the drip could be removed. Peggy

Fry was going to have to start doing her job.

'There you go Mr Choi; I told you I would do it,' I said quietly to myself.

Since my big operation the sludgy brown concoction had kept me alive and hydrated. Every time I wanted to go anywhere the drip had to be disconnected. If I wanted to go to the loo, shower or exercise with Emma the nurses had to unhook me. What really fascinated me was how long the food took to drain into my system because it took hours for the bag to empty, but now I was set free. The drip had been disconnected for good and Peggy Fry was now going to be used to feed me. For the first day the nurses fed me and then on the second they showed me how to do it myself. I had to pour a fortified milkshake into a plastic beaker. I used a syringe to suck up the contents from the beaker and then attach it to Peggy Fry. I would have to open up the tube by releasing a clamp and then push the syringe so the milkshake went directly into my stomach. I would close the clamp, take more milkshake, fix the syringe, open the clamp and dispense the food into the tube. After all the liquid was in I had to flush the tube with water. It was essential the proper sequence was followed. Once I made a mistake and forgot to clamp the tube when taking off the syringe and the milkshake came back up Peggy Fry and poured all over me, the chair and the floor. I never got the sequence wrong again. After I was fed I had to clear up, throw things away and wash the equipment. It all seemed such an unnecessary and complicated palaver for such an unsatisfying feeding experience. I could not taste the milkshake or even enjoy the sensation of eating. But I hated the smell of the strawberry flavoured milkshake, it made me nauseous and so I only used the vanilla and chocolate versions.

Peggy Fry was also being used now to give me my drugs which were diluted in water. The cannulas in my arms were taken away. I had lost the drip. I was getting to be more independent. I was now free to move around as I wished; my prison sentence was over and I could now be fed through the feeding tube. Thank goodness for Peggy Fry, she was living up to her reputation as a kind old cook and part time nurse.

Now my aim was to get home.

Mr Choi asked my permission to write up what had happened to me as a case study. Of course I agreed because if lessons could be drawn to help other patients it was the least I could do. To give something back was an honour. As far as I could tell, Mr Choi would turn my experience into a presentation that he would use on training courses and at teaching seminars. Later in May 2017, when I was in Florida having treatment, Michelle sent me an email to request photographs of my scars to show at scientific seminars and clinical meetings. To help improve his David Bailey skills John took the photographs and we gladly sent them to London. Michelle said I was 'a gem' so I told her to call me Ruby.

One of the best people to observe on the ward was my favourite night nurse who had this wonderful ability to cheer people up. Her humour was infectious. She would have been a tonic on any ward.

Each night at about eight o'clock she would glide into the ward and slide around her patients to enquire how they were. She would roar with laughter at her own jokes and comments and she would wait for us to compliment her on her latest creation, which would sit proudly on top of her head. She had this talent where she would take several headscarves and shape them into exotic headdresses. These headdresses were always different and colourful. Sometimes one of the scarves would be covered in tiny mirrors, so she twinkled as she royally glided around her world handing out her medicine of good humour.

After lights out, she reminded me of a grand old galleon in full sail as she went about her business working efficiently in the shadows.

I would look forward to her arrival on the ward and be disappointed when she was not covering a shift.

Thursday October 27th proved to be an interesting day. This was the day I met my oncologist Dr Beatrice Seddon for the first time. John and I went over to the new Macmillan Cancer Centre, just off Tottenham Court Road, in an ambulance. We could not believe how beautiful the centre is. It is like an upmarket hotel with its seating areas, cafe and huge decorative mobile above the reception desk. We went upstairs for my appointment.

Dr Seddon told us the surgery had removed most of the tumour but I would need high doses of radiotherapy to manage the remaining cancerous cells. Dr Seddon recommended I travel to Florida for proton beam therapy. The next step was to ask the receiving centre in Florida if it was possible to treat me and to put my case for treatment forward to the UK Proton Panel so it could be funded by the NHS. Dr Seddon would send the records of my surgery and my MRI images to Florida so the team could decide if I was eligible. The decision on whether I would go would be decided through a two stage approval process, where Florida would say yes or no and the NHS would agree to fund this next adventure. In anticipation, Mr Choi had made sure all my metal work was in the back of my neck so as not to obstruct the proton beams. Now I had to wait until a decision was made, but if I did not go to Florida I would still have conventional radiotherapy in London.

After the meeting with Dr Seddon, I went to meet my Macmillan Nurse who told me to get in touch about anything that might be worrying me. I have John and so have never used any of the support services in London or Florida, but it is comforting to know they are available if you need them. John is a rock and together we make a strong team.

The conversations with Mr Choi were beginning to change. We were now talking about when I might be discharged from the

National. I preferred to say when I might be allowed to go home because I did not want a discharge on top of everything else. I now needed to reduce my pain killers and the tracheotomy hole had to heal more. I thought I might go home on the Friday after my meeting with Dr Seddon, because I was more mobile and I was feeding myself now, but this was too early and I still had some more healing to do, so I spent another weekend on the ward.

The swelling in my tongue was going down and on a trip to the bathroom I finally summoned up the courage to poke my tongue out at the mirror to see what it looked like. I was totally shocked because it was shorter than before and did not stick out far. It was swollen and it was stitched because it had been cut in half. I felt faint; my head went into a spin and I wanted to be sick. I knew my jaw had been cut and broken, which was brutal enough but to have your tongue sliced was totally scary. I looked at the thick black stitches and I wanted them taken out as soon as possible and before I went home. Mr Choi told me I had lost feeling on the right side of my tongue but over time I would get used to it. He doubted the feeling would return.

Before the next weekend I discussed the painkillers I was having with my pharmacists. I asked if the dosage could be reduced. I wanted to get off the painkillers as quickly as possible. I hate taking medicines and am always conscious of becoming dependent on them. We agreed to reduce the dosage of the painkillers from 10mg to 5mg and from six times a day to 4 times a day, but I also agreed to ask the nurses for more painkillers if I needed them at any time.

Changing the dressing covering my tracheotomy hole was a challenge. It was extremely sticky and therefore difficult to remove. Changing the dressing was painful because the dressing took away the skin on my neck. My skin was hot and red raw. My nurse Jo took her time. I had to be laid out flat so the neck brace could be removed. Jo laid out all the equipment she needed on a steel table that had been sterilised. Jo applied a solution to weaken the adhesive and slowly pulled off the old dressing. I gritted my teeth and squeezed my eyes shut. The wound was cleaned and allowed to dry. I felt great relief as my wound and the skin cooled in the air. I lay quietly enjoying the moment. Jo was delighted to see and tell me how well the hole had closed. A new, clean dressing was applied. The neck brace was put back on and I sat up. Over time Jo used smaller dressings as the hole healed and got smaller.

On the morning of my last Sunday on the ward I woke up to what was really happening to me. No one had said recovery would be such hard work or so difficult. At the clinic where I first met the surgical team, the staff had talked about my planned operations, the risks of having surgery and the possible side effects. The operations were almost the easy bit for me. The anticipation had been unsettling and scary. Would I die on the table? Would I end up paralysed? But in reality I just slept and woke up a bit later with a rotten headache. But in truth no one had prepared me for the few months after the operations and information about what a hard slog it would be had somehow gone amiss. This phase was to be my own sluggish, longwinded and 'orrible grind. S.L.O.G.

Recovery was still going to take more time and I would need all the stamina I could muster and I would need to dig deep to find the determination and strength of purpose to get properly well again. Over the last three and a half weeks I had learned to walk and talk again and I had kicked the tracheotomy, drip and cannulas into touch.

But getting over the operations would be the conquest of my own personal Everest. I had reached base camp and was well set up, but the climb ahead loomed in front of me. This was to be a slog full of discomfort, but I would see the top. The challenges were huge.

One of the best things about my time in hospital was my stream of visitors and I quickly learned that friends had come to keep me company and not hear about all the detail of what was going on. When asked I would tell people I was doing and feeling fine, which I was. If I did give people too much detail I became aware they rarely remembered what I had told them and so I stopped. I was simply delighted they wanted to support me and be part of my adventure.

On my last morning on the ward I awoke from a doze to hear my next door neighbour and his wife talking to a dietitian, who was trying in vain to advise them about what to eat when he returned home. The poor woman was losing the battle. She asked him how much he weighed. The wife interrupted.

'Oh don't worry about that luv. I'll soon get him back to firteen stone. A man needs a bit of meat on him to look healthy and manly. Can't be doing with skinny blokes. It ain't natural.'

'God help the NHS,' I said out loud to myself.

6. Insight

'To survive successfully requires great capability and the ability to think.'

Hanif Kureishi

I left hospital on the first day of November and I thought to start a new month on a new note in a new place was a good omen. But getting out of the National took longer than I thought it would. Before I was allowed to go home my tracheotomy dressing had to be changed, all the drugs I would need had to be organised and I had to pack a large supply of my fortified milk shakes in a suitcase. I left with the stitches in my tongue still intact. Mr Choi told me they would need to dissolve on their own and could not be removed. I would now convalesce at home for a few weeks but make regular visits to the National to see how well I was healing.

I was of course hugely grateful for the time I spent in the National; not just because most of Dolores was gone or because I was healing so well but because during this time my strength of character was tested. I grew to understand that having cancer had provided me with opportunities to recognise my strengths. I used my time in the National to explore how I would react to bad news and what had happened to my body during the horrendous and intrusive operations. I became interested and fascinated with what was happening to me and I used these thoughts to grow stronger.

At work I was always challenging myself by using my brain to develop ideas on how the delivery of education and training could be made more interesting, relevant and exciting. I had been privileged to work in teams with imaginative thinkers. Sometimes I had to work extra hard to convince other people to implement new ideas and I often needed to be cleverer than my enemies and the saboteurs who did not share my philosophies. The ideas we developed and the problems I helped solve often required clever and original thinking and at times my brain had to work at full throttle. I was constantly stimulated by what I was doing and fascinated by the challenges. But since retiring, I was unaware how my brain was actually slowing down due to a lack of stimulation. Without cancer I might have simply fuddled and stumbled my way into old age.

But now life had thrown me a massive challenge where I would have to decide how I was going to deal with having cancer. I had two options where I could choose to wallow in self-pity and become a victim or I could refuse to give in.

I decided I would dance with Dolores, but to my tune not hers.

I discovered I was different to some of the patients I met on visits to hospitals who thought their situation unfair, like the man I met from Hertfordshire in the radiography department at the Macmillan Cancer Centre.

I smiled across at him. I did get a reaction but it was neither friendly nor unfriendly, it was a look that said woe is me, life is so unfair, look at me, I am ill.

He told me his story. He only talked about himself and never asked me once how I was. I sat for what felt ages listening to his depressing story. I realised I could not help him and knew he would not benefit from my more cheerful tale. He would think me mad if I told him to try and make the most of what was going on so he could learn and perhaps even enjoy what was happening to him. I went in for my X-ray and when I came out he had gone, which to be honest was a huge relief.

When I arrived home from the National the flat looked great. There were flowers on every surface from friends and I had a stack of get well cards. It was so good to get home. Our flat is a great place to get better because it is really comfortable and there are different places to sit and relax. I was able to read in one room, watch television in another and relax on the bed.

I went to see Mr Choi on Monday November 7th and I came away with loads of positives stuffed in my pockets. A camera up the nose and down the throat confirmed I had healed and the stitches had dissolved. The tracheotomy dressing was permanently removed because the wound had healed. Over the next year the hole would completely disappear and leave no scar. Mr Choi thought I may be able to start eating properly again later in the week, so an appointment was made for Thursday to meet my swallow nurse, to see if I could start to swallow soft foods. If this worked, Peggy Fry would be retired and she could go and live in her house near her sister. But the neck brace had to stay. The spine was still fragile and my body still had to accept the titanium rods and the carbon fibres in the front of my throat. I wanted rid of that neck brace but this was not going to happen for ages. Mr Choi and his staff all congratulated me on how I had recovered from the operations. The speed with which I was healing had never been expected.

The next four weeks were full of activities; I saw my swallow nurse and had visits from a district nurse, a dietitian and a speech therapist.

The district nurse came to change the tracheotomy dressing and rotate Peggy Fry so she did not attach herself to the lining of my stomach. I was always in the shower when she came to see me, but she never minded because there was always someone else she could go and visit while I finished getting ready. Showering was a right palaver now I was able to shower above my neck and get my hair wet. My wounds had healed well but I still had to shower wearing my neck brace, which meant the padding got soaked. I would dry myself and then when I stepped out of the shower the cooled water trapped in the padding would escape and run down my back. John would then change my pads while I sat in a chair holding my neck so my head would not fall off. Getting dressed took ages because I was quite handicapped. I had slowed down.

The dietician made sure I was swallowing water properly and using Peggy Fry as instructed. One of her jobs was to weigh me. This lovely young lady took her time and through our chats she appeared to be monitoring my wellbeing. I enjoyed our times together.

I was not sure why the speech therapist came to see me because I thought I was speaking normally again. I just assumed she had to report back to the National about my progress and I enjoyed her visits where we talked about how I was feeling.

We went to the National as arranged to see my swallow nurse who wanted to see if I could swallow soft foods. We started with yogurt and progressed to a banana, which was good news because I could now eat the sort of soft chew foods on the list I was given. I asked if Peggy Fry could be removed but the swallow nurse told me this would be Mr Choi's decision.

Over time my health visitors would make fewer visits until before Christmas they stopped all together. I was a bit sad about this, but they told me it was as sure sign I was making great progress.

One thing about my ordeal was how old friends came back into our lives. Since being home an old friend of John's got in touch and he visited us on the first Tuesday. We filled each other in on the years we had lost between us. It was fascinating to find out what had happened to people. Friends had become grandparents, made fortunes, lost fortunes, divorced, remarried, finally accepted they were gay, built businesses, changed careers, experienced illnesses, retired and moved away. Pauline kept in touch with people we had known at college through Facebook. They all lived outside London and so did not visit, but they wrote cards, letters or sent me emails. For those people I did not have email addresses for I sent a Christmas newsletter to tell them what had happened. These friends told other friends and now people I had been at school with and others with whom I had worked got in touch. Letters and cards arrived and people gave me their email addresses. Friends from school, college and my many jobs were back in our lives. The grapevine had done its job. I will need to rent the Albert Hall if we ever have a future party to celebrate. I also discovered friends in Ireland were lighting candles for me. I am one hundred percent sure that Dr Stewart was right when he advised me to tell people I was ill. The love I got back from all these people from different parts of my past life definitely gave me the strength to look Dolores in the eye and tread on her toes.

I was a bit surprised about some people who did not contact me. If I had been asked to make a list of the people who would and who would get in touch once they found out about my dance with Dolores, it would have been wrong in all sorts of ways. In some cases I was surprised and delighted who did make the effort, but I was even more surprised about who I never heard from again. I did not mind being dropped; I was just surprised by who dropped me.

Being at home without all the distractions of the Victor Horsley ward gave me space and time to sit and think and invent mind games. Getting ready in the morning took time but I would often end up sitting in my chair looking out the window. London was in the full grip of autumn and the trees had nearly rid themselves of their leaves. I would sit watching the leaves drop from the huge London plane tree in our garden. Over a couple of weeks I became obsessed by one leaf that clung and refused to fall. It had been left on its own at the end of a branch. On windy days it would spin around violently in circles, but it refused to budge. Each morning I would check to see if it was still there. I tormented myself and decided it would be a good omen if it ended up being the last leaf to fall that autumn. I decided if it was to be the last leaf to fall I would be okay.

After thinking about this risky gamble I decided to improve the odds a bit by adding another ending, where should the leaf not be the last to fall from the tree, then I must at least see it fall.

My rational side told me nothing bad would actually happen, but I was using a deep seated superstition somewhere buried deep inside me to foolishly gamble with my future by listening to the voices in my head and pitch myself against nature. It was as if I was trying to punish myself for the charmed life I had led before the cancer. If I won the gamble my charmed life would continue and I would get better.

As I sat watching my leaf I had time to think about how the cancer had impacted on a life with no breakages. I had not led a fractured life. Before the cancer John and I worked hard to keep our life together simple and uncomplicated. Unlike some people we knew, we did not have fractured lives and worked hard to either avoid or manage problems. But some friends seemed to like their problems and could only function because of them.

One particular friend had so many problems I doubt she would be able to list them all if she were asked. There were so many she could not possibly have remembered them all. She had four children who all gave her headaches in their own ways. Her daughter Sarah ran off with a musician at a tender age and led a bohemian life up North somewhere. One of the sons was withdrawn, but he did go to school where he was bullied. Another son, like his father was a great sportsman but he hated school and was often in hospital with a broken limb and the like. Her fourth child caused no problems at all. Her husband had affairs and eventually they divorced. He remarried but every time I went to see her he was there doing jobs like cutting the grass or fixing the car. Her elderly mother had been over indulged by my friend's father and as a result was spoilt and very demanding of my friend's time. She also had a sister who was going through a terrible divorce. My friend took it on herself to carry her burdens and have her over for weekends.

Whenever I met her she was of course always late because her life was so chaotic and disorganised. If I met her for a drink after work she would talk and I would listen.

'You know Clive is waiting to hear if he has got into the first eleven. If he doesn't get picked I don't know what he'll do. His father says he will because he did.' I didn't know what the first eleven was but I did not want to interrupt her flow.

'Did I tell you his new wife rang me and accused me of trying to get him back? As if? He was only putting up a shelf for fucks sake.

'My sister was over again for the weekend. Lazy cow didn't even make a cup of tea. I was worked to a frazzle, but I do love her. I found a new recipe for lamb, which I'll do for you next time; it's gorgeous. Poor thing; I'm convinced she is about to have a breakdown and of course mum's no use at all. And she's playing up again. She says she wants to come on holiday with me and the kids to Greece.

'Sarah is coming home to see me next week. She says she has something she wants to tell me. I suppose the spotty man boy musician of hers has got her pregnant.' Her phone rang and she walked away to take the call.

'I'll have to go. Clive is in emergency with a broken finger. Sorry darling. I'll phone you,' and with two kisses she went off to sort out another problem and enjoy her chaotic life. I just imagined the fun she would have if Sarah was actually pregnant. I was exhausted and still not up to date with what was happening to the shy son. It was during meetings like this I promised myself I would do everything to keep my life simple and problem free.

John and I knew that even though some friends moaned about their lives they would not change a thing. We were sure these friends even created some problems themselves because they enjoyed the chaos. We were the opposite, where any problems were sorted out. I knew John would not indulge me for long if something was worrying me. We would talk it through and decide what to do about it. I knew some friends thought we could be a bit brutal sometimes and they decided the way we dealt with things was not for them, but it worked for us. Strangely, when talking with friends about their problems I would listen rather than give them the hard advice I would give John or myself. Our approach to organising our lives and how my schooling had taught me not to look at things in an obvious way was helping me choreograph my dances with Dolores.

The leaf on the London plane outside my window was not the last to fall that autumn, but I did see it fall from the tree and so I was safe and all would be okay, except perhaps when I would find something else to gamble my future with. I jumped up from my chair to see where the leaf would land but in the dim light of a late dull and wet November afternoon it just got lost in all the other thousands of leaves lying on the grass waiting to be picked up by the gardeners.

I was walking better now and even went out to cafes for coffee with John, but I did have a bad day when I had to ask Meryl not to visit. I had a vertigo attack and felt awful. On another day I had to cancel Howard for the same reason. I was having good days and bad days.

The stitches in my tongue came away when we were watching a film on the television one Sunday afternoon. It was one of those Sundays in late November when the sky was hung heavy with grey. It was drizzling and chilly. At two o'clock it was already dark enough outside to have lights on. The flat was cosy and we ate nice things and drank tea. The film was Whistle Down the Wind directed by Bryan Forbes and starred Hayley Mills and Alan Bates. This was the first film I had seen as a kid which was not really childish. At the age of ten I remember it had left a big impression on me. It was a mature film with more adult ideas. It was the film that lit up my love for the cinema. Thanks Mr Forbes. I was sitting enjoying the film as much as when I was a kid. I was stretching my tongue around in my mouth when I felt something give. The stitch broke and part of it dissolved. At last my tongue was free. I imagined the broken thread was tickling my throat and I tried to spit it out. There was nothing there. But believe me this stitch had been a thick little baby and it had taken weeks to dissolve. I hated it.

I saw Mr Choi again at the end of November. I was told to keep wearing the neck brace, but was assured I was healing well. There seemed less to be pleased about and it almost felt like I was stagnating except for the fact Mr Choi said the feeding tube could now be removed and asked his staff to make the arrangements. I had been eating soft chew foods for the last three weeks so Peggy Fry was technically redundant, but true to her character she stayed on in case she was needed.

I went to UCLH on the following Friday to Peggy Fry's retirement party. I was grateful to Miss Fry for all she had done for me. She had proved very useful, but it had been bizarre to have a tube hanging out of my stomach. I had always been worried I might cause damage in the night if I turned over or got it caught and I had never really got used to cleaning the area where she entered my body. The nurse in UCLH remembered me from before and made a great fuss of me. Retiring Peggy Fry was nowhere near as difficult as moving her in. The procedure was quite straight forward, but I did sleep for two hours. Poor John sat in the waiting room all this time on a hard uncomfortable chair while I slept in a warm comfortable bed. He had not wanted to go for coffee in case he was needed. I felt bad that I had been so long, but the hospital knew my history with Peggy Fry and they wanted to make sure all was okay with me. I went home with a small hole in my tummy, which healed quickly, but the scar it left would be a constant reminder of Peggy Fry's stay.

On the seventh day of December we got significant news. Florida had agreed to take me on the proton beam treatment programme. Mark from the Macmillan Cancer Centre rang to tell me the team in Jacksonville would be contacting me to confirm dates. He thought I would have to be in Florida for about eight weeks. The NHS would cover the cost of my treatment and our flights, accommodation, car hire and travel insurance. I would have to organise travel visas and insurance, but not until dates were confirmed. Mark could not say when we might leave, but he told me to be prepared to travel to America in perhaps a week's time. We were grateful to be going but we did not relish the idea of being on our own in Florida over Christmas.

After a few emails between Jacksonville and London it was decided we should travel after Christmas to give my neck another month to get stronger. I was still fragile and wearing the neck brace and movement was still extremely limited.

My first contact with Jacksonville was through a lady called Lisa who in a long email told me what would happen. Another email from a lady called Stephanie confirmed the domestic arrangements and my nurse Michelle rang me to introduce herself. Michelle and I chatted for what seemed ages about how much she was looking forward to meeting us and she told me about what the hospital did for its patients. The hospital sounded like a great community and the conversation helped reassure me about visiting Jacksonville. The care Michelle took was wonderful and I felt more confident about the trip.

'Who was that on the phone?' John asked.

'You won't believe who that was,' I replied. I was a bit dumbfounded that I would get a call from a hospital in America to welcome me onto their treatment programme. 'It was my nurse in America, Michelle. She rang to say hello and to see if I had any questions. I couldn't think of any because I was so shocked she would ring. Imagine getting a call like that?'

John was just as impressed as me. The nice young lady at Charing Cross Hospital had rung me to see if I had heard from the National, but apart from appointment booking clerks I never had a call from someone in the NHS to welcome me onto a treatment programme. You have to hand it to the Americans they do know how to add that little extra bit of care. This level of information and contact filled me with confidence. We both agreed the New Year would see the start of a new adventure, but in the meantime we could relax by planning the upcoming festivities.

We always have a great Christmas. You could accurately describe

John and me as a couple of Christmas crackers. We love all the parties and fuss. Christmas for us usually starts when we put up the decorations. We have loads and the flat does look a bit like a winter wonderland or a corner of a New York department store. We cover the fireplace in lights and a huge garland. We have two sets of lights that look like the branches of a tree, which we put in the hall and cover with birds and glass icicles. Then there is the Christmas tree, which is not a mean affair. We hang everything on it and four sets of lights. I would hang myself on it if I could. It takes a whole day to put everything up. One year when I was working, I returned from a visit to Yorkshire to find John had put up all the decorations as a surprise for me. It looked amazing. To celebrate, we sat in the sitting room drinking a bottle of champagne.

'What's flashing in the kitchen? Did you put up lights in there as well?' I asked John. He said nothing and leapt out of his chair.

'Oh my god, I left the frying pan on.' The frying pan was on fire on top of the cooker. John threw a tea towel over it but he forgot to make it wet. Now we had a flaming frying pan and a burning tea towel. We shouted at each other and panicked for a second. He threw me another tea towel to wet in the sink.

'Wet it quick,' John shouted.

'I know I'm not stupid,' I screamed back. I threw the wet tea towel at him and he covered the pan. Together we had dealt with the fire. We did not talk for a few seconds and were relieved it was all over. It took me time to calm down and I could actually feel myself coming down from the ceiling. The problem was solved and the panic over. We were both surprised about what happened because we are always so careful about this sort of thing. But we had learned a valuable lesson. We bought more lights, just for the kitchen.

The festivities normally start with our annual Christmas get together in the private dining room of a posh restaurant somewhere in the West End, but for the first time since my fiftieth birthday Dolores caused me to miss the party because I was just not strong enough. Some friends were supposed to come to the flat to pick up John and have a drink with me on their way to the restaurant, but London was gearing up for Christmas and the roads were packed with cars and so they did not make my little drinks party. John left the flat but he arrived late because of the traffic. I put all the bottles away, tidied up and went for a night in front of the TV; bloody Dolores. Thankfully my friends had a great time.

My first outing was to our friends Gerda and Roger's Christmas party. John told them he would probably be there without me. When I walked in wearing my neck brace they could not believe I made it. John and I agreed we would leave if I got tired or ached too much, but in the end we were among the last to leave. I had a ball. Gerda and Roger know loads of interesting and well connected people and there are always new and fascinating people to meet. One thing about the neck brace is it makes a great talking point and helps break the ice and most people could not believe what I had been through.

On Sunday we went around the corner for my second outing to our friend Anne's Christmas Party. We met Anne through a mutual friend in Leamington Spa. This friend hosted a lunch party one Sunday in a restaurant in the town and he knowingly sat John and me next to Anne. It turned out that Anne lived in the square behind our block of flats. We were neighbours in London and during the lunch we became good friends.

Again Anne knows loads of interesting people. The thing about Anne's party is the food. She cooks for days and the food is always creative and amazing. We kick off the afternoon with Champagne and later move onto her lethal and dangerous Margaritas. Lots of Anne's friends knew I had been in hospital but those who did not were fascinated by the neck brace. Different people asked me if I had had a car accident. I thought the neck brace and a smart suit was not particularly a good look. But I was beginning to discover it does help break ice and is a good talking point. It was a perfect partner to take to parties because it behaves itself and never interrupts. It was a 'Miami J Collar', which could explain why it is not out of place or shy at parties.

We left Anne's in the early evening but we had been there since two o'clock. Without fail the weather is always dry and freezing cold on the Sunday of Anne's party and I always enjoy the short walk back to the flat. For some unknown reason the streets are always quiet and empty, I suspect this is because families are being quiet before the actual Christmas day celebrations. I like the feel of frost on the paths and seeing decorated trees in windows. There is something friendly and comforting about that last Sunday before Christmas, especially helped by the sweet glow left by sour Margaritas. I remembered what Mr Choi had said to me about being dead by Christmas and thanked him and his team I was not dead; I had been to two parties where I stayed until the end and I was getting stronger.

We also managed to have a couple of dinner parties of our own where I made the starters and desserts. Things were looking promising.

We had been invited to spend Christmas in Kingston and Surbiton with Siobhan and Lisa. Until recently John and I had often travelled to Ireland for the holidays, but this had stopped because for three years running we had trouble getting to Ireland due to bad weather.

One year was particularly horrible when we were stranded in Stansted Airport for several hours. When we left the flat to drive to the airport it was beginning to snow, but out in Essex the snow was already beginning to settle and it looked like some planes might be delayed.

When we arrived, the airport was already looking chaotic but we were allowed to check in and pass through security to the departure area. We got a couple of seats which we guarded like a couple of Rottweilers as the terminal filled with more and more people. We were also getting hungry, but all the restaurants were busy and the sandwich bars had huge queues and we did not want to give up our seats. Should we go and eat and loose our seats? Should we wait for news? The situation was getting so bad we could not agree what decision to make? We were convinced that if one of us left to go and get some drinks, the other would lose one of the seats because the crowd was beginning to get ugly and you knew people were becoming more concerned about their own comfort and survival. My fellow travellers were losing their humour and were now beginning to circle other passengers looking for weaknesses. As it went dark outside the terminal was turning into a jungle. Alpha males were becoming protectors of their families.

When our flight was called one alpha male swooped to claim his spot in the forest. I was pleased to escape the chaos of the airport and we agreed to give Ireland at Christmas a miss for a few years.

John's brother Brendan and his wife Teresa were coming over from Ireland for Christmas. They were going to stay with us the night they arrived in London. They had not seen me since our visit to Ireland in June and before all my operations. The doorbell rang. They had arrived. John opened the door. Teresa and Brendan were quieter than usual. They normally make much more noise when we have not seen each other for a while. I stayed back down the hall so they would not see me straight away. I wanted to surprise them. I knew they would be expecting to come across that big blue head. I love a big blue head moment. People are always so polite and a bit tentative. I walked down the hall to greet them. They were shocked to see how well I looked. We sat down and spent a couple of hours catching up over a few drinks.

As would be expected, friends, family and new people I meet always asked me how I feel. It is the first question I am asked every time. I always say I am fine and they ask me why I am so positive. I always shock people when I tell them I have actually enjoyed the experience of being so ill. I tell them I have found being this ill both fascinating and interesting. I know people think I am a bit odd and they look at me in disbelief. But I am totally interested in what happened to me and I am fascinated at how my poor little body healed itself.

I was beginning to view this journey as a privilege. If Dolores had not moved in rent free I would not have discovered how positive I could be or found out what it was like to be looked after by the best people in the business. I put this weird way of looking at my situation down to the fact my brain needs stimulation. Since retiring I have led a quieter life, which meant my life lacked excitement. I was beginning to appreciate how muddling along over the last four years had affected me. But cancer woke my brain up. My brain had been forced to work again and not just hum along on autopilot. My strength of character and my ability to respond positively to Dolores was being tested to the limits. Intellectually I was being forced to look at how I would deal with cancer. This fascinated me. All the bad news and all the decisions John and I had had to make about my treatment, plus all the horrendous physical experiences had actually stimulated my brain so much I had been forced to make sense of my reactions and emotions. Perhaps this is why I was being positive.

Dolores had given me a huge break from my normal and rather dull routines. Most of what we do in life is not madly interesting, fascinating or different. The familiar routines, which we use to organise our lives can dull our emotions and slow down our brains. Perhaps this is why we need to take part in enjoyable or even scary experiences that are novel and different. The art of coping with cancer is to turn something this scary into something novel and enjoyable, which is perhaps bonkers but effective.

All my recent experiences were nothing like I had experienced before and they were concentrating my mind and creating so many strong memories, which would stick with me forever. I did not remember much from the previous four years, so perhaps the brain needs a scare now and then to make our memories more acute, colourful, vivid and memorable.

There was also a conscious and an unconscious side to what was happening to me. I was never quite sure if I had total control of what my brain was doing. It almost felt like my brain was acting on its own. It felt like I had become two people. I was directly in control of a bit of me, which I thought must be my personality, but my brain was responding to the adrenalin rushes independently. The brain was computing ideas and passing them back to my personality so I could cope with and respond to all that was happening to me physically. I often thought my brain was working independently of me so it could help me make sense of all my mixed up and confused emotions.

So having cancer was not a problem psychologically, just physically. The irony was that as I let my brain have free run to develop strategies to help me deal with the cancer I felt more alive than ever. Cancer had woken up my brain. I was enjoying the challenge and having fun. Dolores had turned me into an adrenaline junkie.

Brendan told me I was a conman who had misled people by letting them think I was ill. He could not believe how well I looked, so he could not have seen the big blue head.

The next day was my 64 birthday and I drove us all to Scott and Siobhan's in Kingston as arranged. That evening Lisa and Kevin threw a party for me in their smart new kitchen, which turned out to be a great space for entertaining. Apparently knocking down a wall and creating this new space had been my idea. For some time Kevin and Lisa had wondered what to do with their second living room, which after building an extension had become not much more than a rather large corridor. One Sunday back in the summer people were offering suggestions.

'Why don't you just knock the bloody wall and chimney breast down and have done with it?' I said. I did not remember the conversation. I remembered thinking it would be a good idea, but I could not actually remember suggesting it out loud; perhaps it was when the pain had been particularly horrible, but it had obviously worked even though it had been a huge job.

Lisa and Kevin had asked lots of our friends and I was surprised how many made the journey over to South West London just two days before Christmas. Those who could not make it because they were traveling to families all over the country sent cards for me to open. During the party Kevin and Lisa's little girl called Amelia said she had a headache and even though she managed to play with her cousins I could see she was struggling to keep up. I sang 'When I'm sixty four' by the Beatles. How did I get to be sixty four? This was even more baffling than how did I get cancer. I got lovely presents including an iPad from John's family, which was to prove invaluable in Florida.

We all went into Kingston on Christmas Eve for last minute shopping. When it started to get dark we broke into three separate groups, where some carried on shopping, some of the ladies and kids went off to Mass and the fellas went to the pub. The pub had a fire and Christmas trees and loads of good humoured punters. It was just great getting out again and enjoying the company of friends, especially at such a special time of the year. After the pub we all had a meal together in a restaurant, all three generations of us enjoying each other's company and that feeling that only comes with the excitement of Christmas.

This is what makes my life so worthwhile. I always make out I hate the kids and they call me "grumpy drawers". We sat and talked about Father Christmas and on an iPhone they worked out where he was. The kids started to get a bit agitated when they thought it looked like we might stay in the restaurant longer than was safe because they wanted to get home to get ready for his arrival.

We all spent Christmas Day at Lisa and Kevin's and Boxing Day at Siobhan and Scott's. I did all of Christmas Day, but Boxing Day proved to be a bit too much and I went upstairs in the early evening. I ached now and needed to be quiet. I watched the television and relaxed, but I enjoyed listening to all the excited noise coming from downstairs. I can enjoy listening to people having fun nearly as much as being there. I heard Lisa and Kevin, leave with their kids. The house fell quiet. It almost seemed to shrink a bit as the noise dissipated. John came in and we sat talking about what a great time we were having. We tried to guess when I might stop wearing the neck brace, but my neck still felt fragile and we joked about what would happen if the next morning I forgot to put it on after my shower and my head fell off in front of the kids. Siobhan came in to tell us George Michael was dead. 2016 had been a brutal year where so many of my idols had died. Was I going to get through the remaining few days of 2016 and see 2017? It was a thought.

The next morning John put dry pads in my neck brace after my shower and helped me fit it back on and so did not scare the kids, but Kevin scared us when he rang to tell us Amelia was in hospital. He could not tell us exactly what was wrong but her headache had got worse. We had planned to go home that morning but we hung around waiting for news. The doctors at the hospital could not agree what was wrong with Amelia, even though over the last three weeks Kevin had taken her into emergency a few times. Amelia was moved to St George's hospital in Tooting where the doctors discovered she had a bleed on her brain. After treatment to relieve the pressure, she stayed in hospital to recover. No one was really sure what caused the bleed but a month earlier she had been playing when she fell and hit her head and during one of the last days at school before Christmas she was hit on the side of her head by a ball. Even though falling over and being hit by a ball is not great, John and I thought this was better than having weak arteries that might one day haemorrhage and cause long term problems.

John and I had been invited by Justin and Alan to spend New Year in Seaford. We were not sure if we should go but Lisa and Kevin said there was little we could do and so insisted we spent time with our friends before leaving for the States. Neil and Nichola drove us down and we planned to come home on New Year's Day to give us time to get ready for our American adventure. We thought Neil and Nichola were returning to London as well, but it turned out Neil had already planned to drive us home and then return to Seaford. If I had known of this secret plan, I would have driven to Seaford in our own car. But this is another example of how kind friends are. Imagine, Neil drove all the way to and from London on damp, misty and murky roads. It was dark when we got back to the flat and he had to drive all the way back to the south coast. Nichola insisted this was nothing and told me I would do the same. I probably would.

Despite having to wear that bloody neck brace, New Year was lovely. We bought a huge leg of lamb from our favourite butcher in the town, visited a fabulous shop where a lady sells everything from mirrors and vintage clothes to unusual jewellery. We sat in her shop and chatted about her stock. We finished off the afternoon in the Wellington Arms, which is a comfortable cosy old place, where we had our first drinks to kick off the festivities. After our drink we walked down to the pebble beach and got blown to pieces, which reminded Nichola and me we had not seen the lady with the wind problem this year.

We walked back to the house and set about preparing our evening meal. John was in charge, ably assisted by Nichola. We left them to it and sat down with a drink in the sitting room. It got dark and we sat in a cosy warm house. Like the cast of Downton Abbey we made a big thing of going up stairs to dress for dinner. We all looked smart and ready for a good time. I heated some nibbles I had made to have with our drinks. The temptation is to eat too many and spoil your dinner, so I kept some back for the next day. The meal was gorgeous and unlike the Crawley's of Downton Abbey we all mucked in to serve the dinner and clear the dishes.

The lamb was as good as it looked and John's famous roast potatoes were great. We watched the fireworks from London on the huge television and sang in the New Year. I became a bit pensive and wondered what 2017 would be like? Florida was looming and the promise of another adventure was starting to rattle my nerves. But the omens looked good. As Mr Choi had promised, I had made it through to 2017, unlike so many of my heroes such as David Bowie, Alan Rickman, Prince and Victoria Wood. Even in the last week of what had been a tumultuous year we said goodbye to Debbie Reynolds and her daughter Carrie Fisher and of course George Michael. Then to top it off another name was been added on the last day of the year. The actor

William Christopher who played Father Francis Mulcahy in the hit sitcom M.A.S.H died at his home in Pasadena, California. But he was 84. I set myself a target to reach seventy four but thought again and set it at seventy five because it sounded a bit more optimistic.

7. Adventure

'Travelling – it leaves you speechless, then turns you into a storyteller'

Ibn Battuta

When we got back to the flat after the New Year in Seaford, we only had a couple of days to take down the Christmas decorations, get the flat organised, do our paperwork, pack for our three month trip and say goodbye to friends. The beginning of 2017 was proving to be exhausting.

Neil came to the flat to take us to the airport. During the journey I did not say much. I looked out of the window and wondered if I would miss the winter we were leaving behind. I have never liked the English winter landscape, which to me always looks so dead, dull, drab and dirty. The roadsides are always grubby because the frosts, snow and fogs work together to build banks of light mud and discolour the kerbs. The bare tree branches stand out against a cold blue or stuffy low and depressing grey sky. Before I was ill I had thought it might be great to go and live in Southern European for a month in the winter. I imagined John and me living in a top floor apartment of an old stone building in a medieval city overlooking the Mediterranean. I had thought how lovely it would be to go out for coffee and visit museums, eat tapas and drink wine. This was a day dream I would hang on to because it might help sustain me until it became a reality sometime in the future.

On the journey to the airport that late morning in early January the weather was bright and cold and the branches made the sun flash across the car. I expected Florida to be very different. Would it be warm and sunny as I would expect? Would the trees be green? Did I need the thick warm jacket I was wearing? Would the proton beam therapy work? Would I be able to cope with the long journey ahead?

We arrived at the airport. Neil insisted on parking the car and coming in to help us check in. When we found which line to join in all the confusion that is Heathrow we insisted Neil leave us and go back to Nichola. John stayed in line, but I was beginning to ache and needed to sit down. There were no seats in the check-in area but I spotted a broken office chair, which had been discarded against a wall with a pile of cardboard boxes. The seat was broken but it did the job. I half expected someone to come over and ask me to move but several airport workers who walked past me just smiled and wished me good day as they used a door behind me marked staff only. I think I had been saved by the neck brace. Then an older man came towards me.

'Here we go. Here comes the jobsworth. He won't care about my neck. I don't suppose he'll even notice something is wrong,' I said to myself out loud but in a whisper.

'Good morning sir. Are you okay there?'

'I can't stand for too long; I needed to sit for a bit due to my neck,' I explained. He nodded and went through the staff only door. He returned with a better unbroken chair for me to sit on. I could not thank him enough. When John got to the front of the queue I went over to join him. By the time we had checked in I looked over to see both chairs had been removed. I wondered if they had been removed because I had broken a health and safety regulation.

We went through to departures and settled ourselves in the

lounge for a couple of hours using John's platinum membership card. We were able to relax here and get away from the frantic life of the terminal. I sat and pondered the word terminal and hoped it was not a bad omen. The flight was okay. Only okay because it was economy and I know my neck would have preferred to be at home. The food was awful and we only had wine to drink. I could not concentrate on the films even though the choice was enormous. I turned to the music channels instead and listened to lots of George Michael songs which subdued me. As we got further across the Atlantic people started falling asleep but it was daytime and my head would not let me. I passed the hours just thinking about what had happened. I was not being self-indulgent and I was not feeling sorry for myself. I was just going through the facts and I made sense of it all by putting in sequence all the events of the last few months. If I made a mistake and got an event out of order I went back and started again. The time easily passed.

We landed at Miami where we needed to change onto another flight up to Jacksonville. The walk to the next flight took ages. We could not believe how far we had to walk and were surprised how dated and old fashioned Miami airport looked. So many airports in the UK have been updated and turned into huge commercial shopping malls that boast designer shops and restaurants owned by celebrity chefs. Visits to some British airports have become part of the holiday experience. We arrived at the gate for our next flight but we had over two hours to kill so we had a coffee and a sandwich. Sadly the coffee and sandwich were disappointing. We made it last as long as we could without looking desperate, which of course we were by now. Desperate that is to arrive in Jacksonville.

We arrived in Jacksonville nineteen hours after leaving Heathrow. On the same day two librarians in Lake County, Florida were accused of creative accounting practices. The librarians had invented fake patrons, who they had given false addresses and drivers' licence numbers. Their aim was to make out these bogus patrons took home unpopular books so they would remain on the shelves and not be removed and destroyed. One of the dummy borrowers was Chuck Finley, a retired major-league basketball player, who according to records had read 2,361 books across a wide range of genres from Cannery Row by John Steinbeck to Why Do My Ears Pop? by Ann Fullick. I decided it would be fun to mix with locals who could be that inventive.

As far as we were concerned we had landed in the right place because we thought Boston and Switzerland might be too cold this time of the year. Jacksonville in Florida had more promise but we felt strangely unsettled and I was so tired I did not really remember the drive from the airport or arriving at the new apartment. The next morning I needed a distraction from what was going to happen later.

Sitting up in bed I inspected my ankles. Propped up on pillows I had a good view. For a sixty four year old guy they were in good shape. Only five months earlier they had been fatter and looked like they belonged to someone who was ageing. Now the bones were sticking out they looked young again. I was pleased with the change. Perhaps such a dramatic weight loss was not so bad after all.

I could hear John making tea in our new kitchen. I looked out of the window and it was still dark. We looked over a car park and I could see people leaving for work. In the near distance beyond the car park I could make out a man taking his dog for a walk in a fenced off area barely lit by the new dawn. The dog was making use of the patch of grass, which the developer had provided for doggie business.

The doctors in London had not been worried about my sudden weight loss because they had been pleased with my level of fitness, which they told me was impressive for my age. John brought in the tea. In London we always have two biscuits with our tea to start off the day. We did not have any biscuits because when we arrived the night before the shops were closed. We had brought some tea bags with us and had stolen a few little pots of milk from the airport café in Miami. We might have had biscuits if the catering on the aeroplane had not been so stingy.

'I wonder what today will be like, I wonder what will happen?' I mused. 'I know I have the timetable of meetings and I know who we are going to see and when, but what will they tell me and what will they be like?'

'Don't worry, we'll cope, we always do,' I knew John was right because together we are strong. John is my greatest asset. He has looked after me and given me all the support anyone could wish for. John was right of course about coping. We had successfully coped with so much horrible and shocking news and information over the last seven months because we always talk about everything and never shy away from difficult problems.

A car was coming to pick us up at eight o'clock, which we had arranged to meet at the main gate. It was surprisingly cold and we needed our padded jackets. I had assumed we would wear shorts and polo shirts. It was a beautiful morning and the sky was putting on a dramatic show. The black night sky was being chased away by a confident and vivid orange dawn. I had not seen such a deep strong orange colour before. We were both stunned by the combination of the cold and the beauty. We waited for the car to arrive. By ten past eight I was beginning to worry about being late for my first appointment. We had only been away from London for about a day and half but in the confusion and fear of adjusting to a new but temporary life in Florida, our life in London already felt distant and difficult to remember.

'I'd better go and ring the company. Perhaps the car has broken down,' I said. John agreed and so I went back to the apartment to use the landline. It was a long walk. I had to wait for the lift and the walk down the corridor to the flat was longer than I had remembered. I was beginning to panic. I rang the number on the business card. It went to answerphone. I left a message. Why did no one answer? My stress levels were getting worse. I got myself a drink of water and decided to try one more time. The guy on the phone was full of apology. They had forgotten to send the car but he said one was already on its way. By the time I got back to the gate the new day was dulling the street lights and they began to go off. A big smart black shiny limousine came quickly down the road towards us. I prayed it was ours. The driver was the coolest dude I had ever met. He rolled out of the car full of calm. He drawled his apology sluggishly in a deep Southern American accent and assured us it was not far to the hospital. He pulled out onto the main road and we slowly made our way to route 95. When he got onto the motorway the driver changed into a speed junkie and we overtook every car in front of us. We got to the hospital on time thanks to his driving skills. Nothing seemed to faze this guy and he told us to give him a ring when we were ready to leave.

Our first meeting at the hospital was with an administrator who explained the rules. I signed a paper to confirm I would not sue the hospital if something went wrong. The cancer clinic is part of a teaching hospital attached to the University of Florida. Teaching hospitals cannot be sued. I was pleased to sign the document.

The second meeting was with Michelle, my wonderful nurse. Over the following months Michelle was to become a great friend with whom we would share loads of stories. The three of us hit it off straight away. Three minutes into the meeting and we were all laughing at John's stories. Michelle told us what would happen and that we would have weekly reviews with her to make sure I was okay and everything was going as planned. I was promised a mobile phone and a satnav for our hire car. We were given information about places to visit in Jacksonville and advised about where to shop and eat. The whole experience was turning into an adventure and I was falling in love with everybody at the hospital.

The third meeting was with Dr Rotondo. Dr Rotondo is the most charming and caring man. He always gave us all the time we needed and he was totally responsible for planning and delivering all my treatment. He would work out the strength of radiotherapy I would need. Every proton patient is different and each treatment plan has to be unique. Dr Rotondo told me I would need to have an MRI scan which he would use to plan my treatments. He explained that designing my treatment plan would take about two weeks, during which time we would be free to explore Jacksonville and the surrounding area at our leisure.

Then Dr Rotondo gave us a full briefing, which he told us he would deliver in three parts.

He first told us that I was in Florida to mop up the residual cells left in my spine following my two operations. The aim was to control the growth of what is a slow growing tumour. The protons would deliver high doses of radiation that would be focused on the pocket where the cancer had grown so that other healthy cells would not be destroyed or affected. The treatment would need to be highly specialised because I had a particularly nasty type of Chordoma. One in a million people may develop a Chordoma, but only one in seven million people might develop the rare type of Chordoma I have. So far so good, but now I was in for the bad news.

Dr Rotondo got onto part two and went through the possible side effects I might suffer. 'As you go through your treatment you might feel tired and you could feel listless. Fatigue is usual,' he warned me.

'Okay that does not sound so bad,' I said.

'You could experience something similar to severe sunburn where your skin becomes inflamed. Your throat may be sore and you can expect to have a dry mouth which may lead to your voice becoming hoarse. If this happens, you will find talking difficult. This stage can be particularly horrible.' I did not make a reply this time; I did not know what to say. 'But if this was to happen it will probably happen over the first three weeks and we will control the discomfort for you. We can manage this with targeted pain relief,' he continued. I could feel my throat going sore already and so only nodded to preserve my voice. I was beginning to regret signing the papers I had been given earlier. No, I was beginning to regret boarding the aeroplane at Heathrow and that tiring nineteen hour journey. I was not sure I wanted him to get onto part three.

During part three of the briefing I started to look for an open window through which to jump. 'In the long term you could lose your hair, your skin may become very dry and you may experience changes to your voice,' he went on to tell me. It was unthinkable I would lose my crowning glory of thick grey hair and the late singing career I had promised myself would be over before it had started.

'In later life the effects of the radiation may lead to the growth of additional tumours, but this would probably not happen for between another ten or fifty years.'

That's not so bad then,' I said. 'I'll be one hundred and fourteen in fifty years, which should break a few records.'

'You could over time also lose control of your bladder, have problems with swallowing and so may have to be fed by a tube. Your bones may become brittle and you could suffer from bone fractures and may have problems with your spinal cord.'

'Anything else I should worry about?' I asked weakly.

'Yes. You could die of course,' he concluded.

While Dr Rotondo was telling us all this I kept clinging to particular words he used like 'may' and 'could'. So nothing was exactly definite and they were only risks and chances. I knew I was odd and different and even perhaps an alien from another galaxy, so I was hopeful. We discussed the long term effects further and Mr Rotondo made me feel a bit better about the whole process.

'The Chordoma would more than likely cause the same problems if it is not kept in check and in reality the risks of the treatment are lower than the risks caused by the tumour itself, which if left untreated will kill you anyway,' he told me. Armed with this information I decided the option to go ahead with the proton was better. I did not regret getting on the aeroplane in Heathrow or the tortuous journey after all.

Now I knew how unusual my case was and how rare my tumour was I was delighted to give my agreement for the university to use my data for research purposes. I was getting used to being a case study.

After all this Dr Rotondo gave me a physical examination where, amongst other things he tested my reflexes and strength. He thought I was physically very well and he told me I was the king of recovery, especially when he considered the severity of my surgery. But we did discover I had a drop foot because I could not walk on my right heel. He did not think this would change, but I would make it my mission to get rid of this drop foot. I would exercise it. He asked me to think about losing the neck brace. We agreed I would take it off a few times a day but would wear it when out in public places as a warning to other people not to knock into me or worse over. Even though I had been waiting to be told to lose it, the thought made me feel a bit nervous, but I could not wait to have my first shower without it.

We thanked Dr Rotondo and Michelle who told us they would be in touch in a couple of weeks to confirm the start date for my treatment. We went back out to reception for a short break and a cup of coffee. The next job was for me to be fitted with a mask that would help me keep still during treatment and help the radiologists pinpoint the proton beam therapy on what was left of Dolores.

John looked absolutely drained and he went to talk with Gerri, the fabulous receptionist. Gerri asked him if he was okay. He asked Gerri if she had a gun. Gerri looked a bit shocked at first until John joked he wanted to shoot himself after being given such a long list of scary information. He told her he was a bit shocked about what we had just been told and joked that he might as well shoot me and himself now and so get the whole thing over and done with and save the NHS some money. Requesting a gun from a Floridian is not the best idea. We found out later to never ask an American if they have a gun. They might just hand you one.

After our break Michelle came looking for us to take me to the torture chamber. I changed into a hospital gown and was taken into the room with a CT scanner where I was introduced to three charming ladies who, over the next forty five minutes would manipulate and torture me. Their first job was to fit me with a mask and this was to be the first test to see how I would get on not wearing the neck brace. I took of my neck brace and lay on the table and I was fitted with sheepskin wrist restraints. I called them my handcuffs. The handcuffs were each fitted with canvas straps which were attached to a board shaped like a triangular cloche. Wearing the handcuffs I bent my knees, put my feet on the triangular cloche and pushed it away by straightening my legs so I was stretched out in a straight line. I lay on a solid plastic pillow that was shaped to fit the back of my head. The pillow had studs along the back, so when the mask was made it could be attached to restrict my movement and keep me still. A mouth guard was pushed into the front of my mouth which I was told to squeeze with my teeth. I started to gag and my eyes watered. I was told to wrap my lips around the front of the guard while one of the ladies placed a heated plastic sheet over my face. She attached it to the mouth piece and then pushed it down on my face so it was moulded to the shape of my profile. I breathed deeply to stop being sick, control my breath and manage the feeling of claustrophobia. The plastic sheet took on a smell when it warmed. It smelled of warm oats. Not long now, I was reassured. The three ladies pushed and shaped the mask around my face, the back of my head and neck. The mask was taken off and holes were made for my eyes, nose and mouth. It was much easier to bear with the holes.

I joked with the ladies that if I wanted to wear handcuffs and be fitted with a mask in London it would cost me a week's wages. They laughed with me. But I am sure they had heard it before. Perhaps not, who other than an Englishman like me would think of saying something so bold? I am sure Americans are far too polite to make rude comments.

'I'm from New York,' one of the ladies told me. 'It would cost the same there.' I apologised for the joke. 'Don't you worry about that, coming from New York it takes a lot to shock me. Besides it was a good joke,' she reassured me. It also lifted the mood and I think the three ladies were pleased they could be more relaxed with me. Wearing the mask I had my CT scan.

In addition to the tumour I also had a lump forming on the side of my neck. It was giving me pain now and it looked horrible. It reminded me of an old hearth rug which had rucked up. My skin was rucking up under my right ear and as it rucked it creased and wrinkled into an ugly throbbing mass. No one seemed to know exactly what it was but they were sure it was not a tumour. We found out later it was scar tissue caused by the September and October operations.

The last appointment was to have a blood test to check if I was okay to have an MRI on Monday. We went across to the main hospital for the test and I could not believe the amount of bureaucracy involved. Bureau crazy would have been a better description for what I experienced. A lady with the most amazing finger nails I had ever seen interviewed me for ten minutes to confirm that all the funds were in place for me to have the blood test. Her nails were about an inch long and each nail was painted red and white. The white side of the nail was also decorated with small green, red and blue gem stones.

'I hope you don't mind me saying, but your nails are fabulous,' I told the clerk. 'I have never seen anything like that much detail. They are amazing.'

'Thank you,' was all she said and it was obvious she did not want to take part in small talk. But a colleague came and stood behind her to tell me she loved my accent and hoped to visit London one day.

I experienced the same level of bureaucracy every time I went for a scan, X-ray or blood test. It was no wonder health insurance premiums in America are so high. It occurred to us that a whole industry must have been created to employ armies of administrators who check and recheck insurance policies.

Apart from the MRI scan booked for Monday, we were now free until January 19th when my treatment would start. We now had some time to explore and get to know Jacksonville.

We went back to the cancer centre to collect a sat-nav and mobile phone and order a car to take us to Budget Cars where we would pick up our hire car. Gerri introduced us to Mitch who works at the centre. Mitch is English and originates from Nottingham and his job is to help patients and offer assistance where he can. This charming man then offered to take us to the car hire office.

On the way to pick up our car he did a detour to give us a tour and quick introduction to Jacksonville. He showed us where the good restaurants and bars were. He took us to the old town and showed us where the smart historical homes are and he pointed out museums and other places of interest. He recommended a couple of restaurants including one called the Black Sheep and he told us he loved Jacksonville and the Florida weather. This brief introduction to the centre of Jacksonville was brilliant for me. I now had a good feel for the layout of the city we would need and use. I even now knew how to get to the particular pharmacy I would use to pick up prescriptions.

The lady who runs the car hire office is called Ruth and was just gorgeous and we got to know her quite well over the next few months. Everybody we met in Florida was charming and they could not be more helpful. They are all great ambassadors for their state and country. The car was okay, a pretty bog standard white saloon, but easy to drive. It was a short drive back to the apartment complex where we were living, but it was a bit scary. I was pleased I only had to use local roads and not venture onto Route 95. The trouble was the local roads I used in downtown Jacksonville when we left the car hire company were all one way streets. I did drive one way, but the wrong way. This caused a bit of minor mayhem especially for a lady on a pedestrian crossing who was surprised to see me coming at her from the wrong direction. Two builders in a huge Ford pickup laughed at us and made rude signs; but I was a bit confused because I was definitely not masturbating at the time. I left venturing out onto a freeway for another day. We stopped at the supermarket in front of our apartment and bought a few bits to keep us going. We got back to the flat and decided to stay in and have a quiet night in front of the television. We were exhausted after the events of the last few days.

'What did you make of what Dr Rotondo told us today?' I asked John. I knew what we had heard had bothered him and I guessed it must have been playing on his mind.

'You know I asked Gerri for a gun didn't you,' John answered. 'I could not believe what he told us, but he didn't say it would all happen, he just told us what could or may happen.'

'Yes I suppose he was going through the motions.'

'I think they always tell everybody the lot. Perhaps they think it is better to warn people and to put them totally in the picture. We'll be okay. Look how you have dealt with it all and how well you recovered,' John tried to reassure me.

'Litigation is big over here so I suppose they tell you everything so they can't be sued. I signed the papers and they can always say I was fully informed.'

'You wouldn't sue anyway would you?' John asked.

'Why would I sue people who are doing all they can to help me. If they cocked up or were negligent I might ask a few difficult questions. Unless I'm dead,' I replied.

We finished the unpacking and settled into our new home. We loved the flat which was an unusual shape because it was in the space where the two halves of the building met at right angles. The two bedrooms were on either side of an open plan living area, which occupied the middle of the flat and included a full fitted kitchen and separate sitting and eating area. Tucked behind the kitchen was a neatly designed utility room with a washing machine and dryer. The seating area looked out on a large balcony, which sadly only got the sun at first dawn. Each of the bedrooms had a bathroom and walk in closets, which I had never seen before. I thought the walk in closets were brilliant and such a touch of luxury. The flat was also very well furnished. After a couple of days living in the flat we moved the furniture around a bit to make it a bit more practical. When we used FaceTime to talk to family and friends back home we always gave them a tour and raved about the layout of the flat and of course I always wanted them to see the walk in closets.

The flat had been such a great part of the trip. When it was first suggested back in London we might have to go to Florida, John and I thought we would probably end up staying in a motel room. Unsure of what would happen we even talked about booking our own accommodation. When Stephanie from the hospital told us where we were going to live in her email back in December we were more than relieved and surprised, especially after I looked up the complex on the internet. Before this I had visions of living in a rundown motel on a main road junction. I had imagined a busy road, low flying aircraft, polluted air, a flashing pink neon sign, dirty 1950s décor which included sticky carpets, peeling paint, broken venetian blinds, nylon sheets and standing on a wood effect Formica top in the corner of the room an electric hotplate on which to cook. The flat was not of course straight off the set of Dynasty. It was more like something you might see on Breaking Bad, but to our relief we would not be living in a room straight out of a Quentin Tarantino movie surrounded by sinister drug dealers.

The flat had a good view of a beautiful railway bridge that spanned the huge St John's River. As a grand piece of engineering the bridge fascinated me as it rose up and down on a hydraulic system to let boats sail further up the river. I was always looking to see if it was up or down and the trains made a great noise when sounding their hooters as they approached the bridge. The sound was nostalgic and I imagined myself back in the forties on the set of a classic Hollywood film. The sound summoned up pictures of steamy Florida weather where an escaped convict would be hunted by corrupt policemen and a pack of bloodhounds through swampy marshland. The convict would later be saved through the efforts of a handsome Gregory Peck dressed in a crumpled beige linen suit.

It was another cold day on Saturday and we decided to go out for dinner to one of the restaurants just outside our gated development. They all looked okay so we walked around in the dark reading menus. We chose the tex-mex establishment because the weather was so cold and it was the last one we looked at. We were not going to walk back to one of the other restaurants in such bad weather. A beautiful young black man was working on reception. He realised we were from England. We told him we could not believe how cold it was.

'Cold. You think it's cold? You should be me? I hate it. It's so cold I'm scared. I'm always scared when it gets this cold in Jacksonville. We ain't used to it babes. Florida's supposed to be hot. It's scary,' he screamed in a loud, slightly camp and slow southern drawl which just added to the drama of our introduction beautifully. He took us off to our table. 'Now you make sure you have a good time with us. Your server will be over directly to take your order.' With this he turned on one heel and danced off ready to greet the next diners. We loved him.

The restaurant had six huge television screens over the bar. Each screen was showing a different type of sport. There was golf, baseball, boxing, motor racing, soccer and American football. The sound on each television was on, so there was a cacophony of noise which the customers had to shout above. The manager asked us what we wanted to drink. We ordered a bottle of wine. He brought it over with two beautiful glasses. He saw our surprise at the glasses and pulled our legs by asking us if we were expecting plastic cups. He assured us he had a lot of class. We all enjoyed the banter and he went out of his way to look after us. He even moved us to a spot in the room that was a bit quieter. He told us he really wanted to visit London one day. He and the receptionist both received a good tip. The walk back to the flat was brisk.

On Sunday we went to see what St John's shopping centre was like. Michelle had told us it was a good place to visit because it had loads of places to eat and there was a cinema nearby. We were travelling along the freeway quite nicely. The satnav was doing a good job and the roads were not too busy for my first outing on Route 95. Then something unplanned happened. The freeway ahead of us was closed for maintenance and we had to exit at the next slip road. There were bollards everywhere topped with flashing orange lights. The lanes were quite narrow and I got disorientated. At the bottom of the slip road you had the choice of turning left or right. I needed to turn left, which meant crossing a major three lane trunk road. As I approached the traffic light at the bottom of the slip road it turned from green to red but it was not that safe to stop and so I went over a slightly red light.

In the confusion I did not take proper stock of where I was and I turned left, as I would do at home. I should have taken a wide sweep across the three lanes of traffic on my left to get over to the right side of the trunk road. For that split second I forgot Americans drive on the right. I did not take a wide sweep and the car was now facing three lanes of oncoming traffic. The lights changed to green and the mass of cars moved towards me. I was in their way. I knew I was in the way because John started screaming but no one in the facing cars panicked or got angry. They were all very patient and understanding and they gave me plenty of time to calmly back up, turn the car and move out of their way. We were safe and I thanked the heavens that Americans are such great drivers.

We walked around St John's and had a quiet coffee and cake to calm our nerves. To avoid any other mishaps, I even parked the car at the far end of the car park away from other cars. But we did get another shock when we did not get any change out of the twenty dollar bill I handed the server to pay for the coffee and cakes. But unlike at Miami airport it was good coffee this time and we always made a habit of having coffee there every time we went to St John's. We only made a short visit this time because I could not walk long distances yet. I was still recovering from the events of September and October and wearing the neck brace meant walking around was hard work. It would be some months before I could do more strenuous activities.

Monday arrived and we took ourselves off to the hospital for my MRI scan. We drove to the hospital in the footsteps of our cool dude which meant we travelled up Route 95, which was busy with commuter traffic. The cars were traveling fast, and unlike in England all the cars in each lane were all traveling at the same speed. The journey was scary. As the road swooped north, our journey took us high above the city on massive flyovers and I had to cross over to the right so we could turn off for the hospital, but this meant having to cross six lanes of traffic at high altitude. The combination of packed roads, fast traffic, six lanes and being high above Jacksonville made me lose confidence and I started to panic. It quickly looked like I was going to run out of road and miss the turning for the hospital. A huge pickup truck flashed me in to the fifth lane and I let two cars pass me in the sixth lane before moving over and then out of nowhere the exit for the hospital leapt up in front of us. I took the exit faster than was comfortable and we rushed down the slip road. I applied the brakes and we joined the traffic coming from the left at the bottom. I now had to force myself over to the far left lane by crossing three more lanes full of cars, lorries, a school bus and pickups. I drove up to the traffic light and turned left into the road up to the hospital. When we parked the car I had to sit for a while to let my heart rate recover.

'Blimey,' I said to John. 'I don't think I can do that every day. Let's hope our appointments are after the rush hour, when the roads are not so busy.' John did not say a thing and could only manage a nod. Route 95 had become my new nemesis.

The scan was done in the main hospital and the MRI unit was not easy to find. It was tucked away down a long corridor. I had thought all hospitals in America would be shiny and new. It was comforting to discover this is not always the case and like at home they can be a bit run down and confusing. It was the same when I had the blood test on Friday because that part of the hospital was even more tatty. We reported to the reception area where I had to produce my passport. I felt sorry for the receptionist because she sat in a dingy, poorly lit room behind a metal grill. I poked my passport through a hole in the grill and she gave me a declaration form to fill in. I wondered what it must be like to sit in the bowels of this huge building in a small space behind a metal grill checking in people for scans. We sat in the waiting room and I filled in the form. While we sat waiting I thought about the journey to the hospital and hoped there was another route back to the apartment because Mitch had driven through Jacksonville and out to the old town when he gave us the tour without going on the freeway. I could drive back via the car hire office but that would be stupid and take us out of our way. There must be a more direct way back to where we were living.

I was called for my scan. We agreed that John should wait for me in the main reception by the front door and not in the small dingy waiting room. I went in for my scan, which lasted one and a half hours.

When I was finished the radiologists agreed with me when I told them I must have been well and truly cooked. The ladies enjoyed the joke but it had been hard for me because of the rods in my neck. I took a few minutes to get myself moving again. When I left I was a bit stiff and John was not waiting in the main reception. He was standing outside the MRI unit in the long corridor looking worried because I had been gone for so long.

We went back to the car and I set the sat-nav to see how to get back. It showed we would have to go back using Route 95. I looked at the skyline of Jacksonville and was sure I could get back without the sat-nav. Using the skyscrapers as landmarks I got us back on calmer local roads. We were now free for a couple of weeks.

We spent Tuesday getting the flat the way we wanted and we did a big shop to make sure we had all the stuff we needed to cook the sort of meals we were used too. We drove to a big shopping centre that we would use on a regular basis. John was a bit surprised by the price of cucumbers.

'Excuse me,' John said to a guy who was filling shelves. 'Are these cucumbers really five dollars?'

'Yes sir,' he replied.

'But I don't want the box, I only want one,' John quipped.

'They are five dollars each sir, but they are organic.' The poor assistant either did not get the joke or chose to ignore John.

We went to the beach on Wednesday. The weather was a bit warmer, but still not warm enough to sit in the sun or even paddle in the sea. The three beaches in Jacksonville are enormous and go on for miles. I was beginning to see how big the USA is, but I was never going to feel comfortable about its size. We found a lovely café and some cute shops set in a warren of pretty streets lined with timber buildings and it had the look of an area you might expect to find in New England rather than Florida. We liked this part of Jacksonville on the coast and over the next few months would often visit to have lunch or a cup of coffee, or simply enjoy the sun and seaside.

When we got back to the flat, I decided to write and thank Mark for making all the arrangements for the trip:

Dear Mark

I thought you might like to hear we arrived safely in Jacksonville and are settling in. The flat is lovely and we have a car. When we first got the car I drove up two one way streets the wrong way. A bit later I jumped a red light and ended up facing three lanes of oncoming traffic. Everyone was dead calm and understanding. I am pleased to say things have improved. I now drive on the correct side of the road and can see the traffic lights! So we have a good chance of surviving this adventure. We met the team last Friday for a briefing and Dr Rotondo went through what can go wrong. SCARY. But we chose not to take it too seriously. The treatment starts on January 19th. I had my MRI on Monday, which took one and a half hours. Dr Rotondo will use the results to develop my treatment plan. John is a big star. He is looking after me and cooks me lovely meals.

It was cold here for four days, but it is lovely now. We went to the beach on Wednesday. The beaches are huge. We had coffee in a little trendy place. $20 for two coffees and two chocolate twists! I nearly fell over. It is so expensive here. I saw a cardigan by Ted Baker on Sunday in a shop. It was in the sale for $200. I bought the same cardigan in London for £60! Food parcels gratefully received!

Thank you so much for organising this trip Mark and all my best wishes.

James

On Thursday it was warm enough to sit by the pool where we were staying. We had the pool to ourselves and I think this was because the other residents thought it was still chilly and we were mad. *Mad dogs and Englishmen go out in the weakest sun.* Coming from a damp cold wintery London in January, we thought it was heaven. I made myself comfortable on my sunbed, took off the neck brace and with the warm sun on my face read my book. After a while another couple, probably in their seventies came and sat by the pool. I thought they might be English and when we only acknowledged each other with a polite nod, I was sure I was right.

For Saturday night we booked a table at the Black Sheep, and because Mitch told us it was the best restaurant in town, John wore a suit and I put on a smart sports jacket and polished shoes. It turned out we were overdressed, but we were flying the flag for Great Britain. We knew this to be true when we left the restaurant and walked around the local streets because two pretty women asked if we were diplomats from overseas. Tee shirts and trainers were obviously the order of the day. Earlier at the restaurant I ordered a fish I had not heard of before but was reassured it was like cod. John ordered the pork chop, which was served on a bed of grits. My fish was well presented and it tasted okay but John's pork was so tough he left it. The waiter came to clear the dishes.

'Would you like a box for the pork chop sir?' he asked John.

'What to bury it?' John answered. The waiter did not get it at all. He was charming but he did not ask why John had not eaten the chop. We had one bottle of wine, we did not have desserts or coffee and the bill was one hundred and forty eight dollars. We were shocked at the price because people are always moaning about what an expensive place London is. The tables did not even boast table linen and the food was a little underwhelming.

We left and went looking for a bar, but they were all crowded and none of them looked that inviting, so we went back to the flat.

On Sunday it was cold again but to get out for a little while we drove to a Sunday market, which had been recommended. Coming from London we are used to huge markets like Portobello Road, Petticoat Lane and the Sunday flower market on Columbia Road. These markets are full of stalls selling all sorts of goods and produce. Portobello goes from antiques to fruit and veg through to junk, jewellery and vintage and gives the visitor two miles of fascination and amusement. Columbia Road with its flowers and plants is full of noise and colour and places to eat. So we were looking forward to a bit of excitement, but our hopes were soon dashed.

There were only twelve stalls spread out over quite a large area of derelict and uneven ground under a huge bridge that carried Route 95 across the wide expanse of the Saint John's River. Two elderly men were selling heads of broccoli out of stainless steel bowls and nothing else. Either their harvest was not that good or perhaps they were just not very good at gardening. It only took us twelve minutes to visit all the stalls. One lady was selling pictures of Jacksonville's famous bridges. These were excellent and I was tempted to buy the painting of the railway bridge I so admired. We walked down to the river front where we got an excellent view of the real thing and we watched it rise on its hydraulics to let a boat pass up the river. We decided to return on another Sunday when it was warmer because we thought it might be busier in warmer weather. I never did buy the picture.

On Monday we woke to a beautiful sunny morning and by lunchtime it was nice and warm so we took ourselves off to the pool and for the first time I left the neck brace in the apartment. It was a bit breezy but we could sit and read. We were joined by the English couple again and this time we got talking. They were over from England to see their daughter who was having proton beam treatment. A little later her daughter and her husband joined us and we swapped stories about MRIs and operations. It turned out they were living in the flat on the second floor below us. They had been more adventurous than us and had visited Orlando. But I was still not able to walk long distances and so thought it would be a waste of time to try.

By Tuesday we had now been in Jacksonville for twelve days and some pennies were beginning to drop. This trip to Florida was not going to be like being on a two week holiday in the sunshine. We were not on holiday. We were here to manage the place where Dolores had been living rent free and we had to work hard to get me better. We had a job to do. We were in this for the long haul.

We were already feeling homesick, a little bit disorientated and more than a bit apprehensive. Our resilience was being tested and we were not sure if we would be able to stay the course or put up with what was ahead of us. The remaining 79 days stretched out in front of us and they seemed more than a lifetime to us.

We had also been warned the whole trip might even extend beyond the original ninety days depending on how well I responded to the treatment. All the unknowns, potential delays and the next seventy nine days made us a bit scared and we both admitted to butterflies in the stomach. But one or two things were improving. Over the last eleven days I had seen an improvement in some of the old 'war wounds' I had collected back in October. I noticed my front teeth did not hurt anymore. I had had pains in my front jaw where the bone was cut during my second operation and the gums sometimes throbbed in a weird and wobbly way. The wounds had healed, the pain was gone and my lips had given up dancing the hula hula. I could yawn and cough again without wincing. The old shooting pains that went across the top of my head had stopped. I also had a lump in my lower lip which was hard. I had called this lump my little ball bearing and during quiet moments would clench it between my teeth to test how hard it was and to see if it was painful. This was now shrinking and would soon be gone. Several blood blisters on my lips and inside my mouth had disappeared without me noticing until one morning when cleaning my teeth I saw they were not there anymore. My body never failed to impress me with how it was recovering from all the traumas. Magically my scars were fading, blisters and pain were disappearing and I was beginning to feel normal again.

Then my new world imploded on me. We were getting nearer the date when Michelle would ring to confirm the start date of my treatment. The phone rang on Tuesday to ask me to go in to see Dr Rotondo the next day at 10 o'clock. We thought this was to agree when my treatment would start but were we in for a shock.

We were shown into a small consulting room. Michelle was on a trip to New York to see her family and so another nurse showed us where to go and said Dr Rotondo would not be long. I started to feel uneasy and began to worry. He came in to give us the news. I was not going to start my treatment because the tumour had grown back. He had discussed what was happening with Mr Choi and Dr Seddon back in London and together they had agreed I had three options. Dr Rotondo said I could go back to London for more surgery, go ahead with the treatment as planned where the delivery of protons would be more limited or try and deal with the growth using traditional radiotherapy. With the second and third options Dr Rotondo would monitor how the tumour was behaving. He said the choice was mine. He told me to go away and think about my options but not to leave it too long. John and I looked at each other and we both knew instantly what to do.

'I don't need time to think about it. I will go back to London and have it removed surgically,' I replied. I knew John was thinking the same. We just had to return to London. The great thing about John and I is that when something is important we always know what the other is thinking.

'This is the best decision you can make,' Dr Rotondo confirmed. 'Mr Choi and Dr Seddon and I agree this is the best and safest option but we wanted you to reach your own decision. We were not sure you would want to go down this route because of all the invasive and traumatic surgery you had last year. We all thought you might not want to do this all over again.'

Dr Rotondo congratulated us and said we had made the best decision and promised to contact London straight away so flights could be organised.

It was January 18th and we flew home two days later on the 20th. We gave away all our food and cooking ingredients to the English couple who lived in the flat below us. Mitch kindly agreed to store other things we had bought to make our stay in Jacksonville a bit more comfortable until our return in a few weeks. It was all a bit of a rush, but we did it. We packed, returned the hire car to Ruth and our cool dude drove us to the airport. We did not really have time to worry about what was going on.

I had to get back to Mr Choi so he could deal with Dolores who had shown herself to be a particularly tough and aggressive old bitch. Dr Rotondo told us it was extremely unusual for a Chordoma to grow back in such a short time.

8. Lungs

'Nurses may not be angels, but they are the next best thing'

Anonymous

I went woozy and wobbly. I started shaking, sweating and my breathing got worse. Then I lost my hearing and could not hear what the staff were saying to me. My eyesight went strange. Everything in the consultancy room went vague, wobbly and watery. People turned into blurred shadows and they looked like I was looking at them from behind a water fall. The doctors and nurses were joined by other doctors and nurses and someone was shouting instructions and people were running around. A needle was pushed into my skin. I could not control my world anymore. My brain started to melt inside my skull. I was deaf and blind and had fallen into a dark sombre world. Then just as suddenly as the fit had started it dissipated and I revived. I could hear noises but I could not make out what people were saying. Their shapes started to take a more solid form again. The sweating stopped. I was covered in a blotchy rash from head to foot. It had been a horrible experience. So horrible, I wanted to take my eyes out of their sockets and give them a good rinse under running water.

The doctors thought I might have had an allergic reaction to the iodine that had been injected into me when I went to have a CT scan. They also thought I may had had a bad reaction to some antibiotics I had been given. They could not be sure.

Earlier I had been wheeled into accident and emergency at UCLH, where a nurse did all the necessary tests so the doctors could make a diagnosis. My blood was taken. I went to X-ray. Then a bit later I went to have that risky CT scan. I had to lay flat and put my hands behind my head. This was tough because lying flat caused pains in my neck. A voice told me when to hold my breath, which was difficult and I wanted to be sick because I could hardly breathe. I prayed for the CT scan to end; I wanted it over. One last deep breath and it was finished.

Back in the consultancy room the doctors told me I had a blood clot on my left lung. They thought it had probably formed in my left leg as a deep vein thrombosis. So I had suffered an embolism.

We had been back from Florida for a week and were looking forward to sorting out Dolores, but this would now have to wait because of the bloody blood clot. Nothing had prepared us for this blip. I had started to feel unwell on Friday when we met Neil and Nichola for a coffee. I was not that cheerful and I had had a pain in my knee and just felt generally run down.

Friday night was better when John and I had a wonderful Chinese meal. It was Chinese New Year so Queensway was cheerful. It's always great to see the streets full of people having a good time and we met a colourful elderly gentleman who sat on the table next to ours. Over the years I had often seen him walking around Bayswater. He was difficult to miss with his dyed raven black hair and extravagant clothes. He might have been a liar or a person with an over active imagination because he seemed to know everybody and passed the time name dropping. He had impeccable manners and made a great effort to enquire about my neck. He took great care rolling a cigarette and seemed to take delight arranging all the paraphernalia necessary for the operation on the table in front of him. He sat nursing the cigarette between his beautiful, but perhaps over manicured fingers, which

I assumed he would enjoy on his slow walk back to his flat.

'Lovely to meet you both,' he said when we stood up to leave. 'And may I wish you every good wish for the future. I'm sure you will be fine. You will no doubt have a few setbacks but all will be good in the end.' I took his best wishes as a good omen coming from such an interesting character who seemed so at home in eccentric and accepting Bayswater.

I still felt unwell on Saturday but we agreed to invite Robert, Neil and Nichola over for dinner. Nichola had suggested we go to the Chinese restaurant and not cook, but we had already had one and it would be near impossible to get a table on the actual day of New Year and so we thought dinner in the flat would be a better option. I easily drove John to the supermarket to get the ingredients for dinner. The evening went well. I ate a huge dinner and drank booze but a little later I started to feel a serious pain on my side. I began to feel awful and fell asleep in an armchair. Our guests understood and did not take much notice of me. The party broke up just after midnight and John suggested I go to bed while he cleared up.

I tried lying down but the pain made it impossible. The pain was terrible. I gave up trying to sleep and sat in an armchair. I did not sleep at all. Nights like this are weird. They are not boring or long. The brain takes on a different way of thinking. My thinking slowed down and I hovered from one subject to the other. The view from the window takes on a more mysterious and bewitching tone and I take comfort from listening to the sounds of John sleeping in the next room.

Every so often the pain caused me distress. The pain was there all the time, but now and then it got angry and rose up to hurt me. I was finding it more and more difficult to breathe. Not being able to breathe was really scary. John came in at dawn and sat with me. I dozed off for a couple of hours.

We were due to have lunch with friends but John decided it might be best to cancel and while he was out of the room he rang the NHS helpline. The lady needed to speak with me. I was even finding it difficult to speak by now.

I was pleased and surprised a paramedic arrived in no time. This chap hailed from Glasgow and in five minutes took complete control of the situation. An ambulance was called. In the meantime Neil and Nichola turned up to pick up their car from the night before after wisely taking a taxi home. They were of course shocked to see the paramedic's car and an ambulance parked outside. I only saw them when I was wheeled out of the flat in a flimsy contraction of a chair wrapped tightly in a red blanket. I had to laugh at how I must have looked. Nichola looked totally shocked. I was made comfortable in the back of the ambulance and off we went.

The paramedics decided to take me to UCLH because it is run by the same health trust as the National where I was due to be treated by Mr Choi. It was also the day a report was given coverage in the Sunday papers by the consultancy 2020health, which claimed one third of Brits delay going to see their doctor in fear of finding out they may have a serious illness like cancer. Ironically, I had been banging on my doctor's door for months to find out what was wrong with me.

All night in the chair I was sure Dolores was causing the pain in my side. I wondered if she had metastasised and was now traveling around my body. I imagined she had travelled south for the winter. She was now living on one of my ribs. She had taken a villa on a cliff in Tenerife overlooking the Atlantic, which I of course was paying for. She had finally got me and was doing her best to finish me off. But Dolores was innocent this time. The doctors told me the blood clot had stopped me breathing properly and because of this my heart was not getting all the oxygen it needed. They were also concerned my lung might collapse. Clots are a serious business. They can cause heart attacks or strokes. To help me I was given oxygen and pain killers that I was told would eventually help me breathe more normally and I was attached to more tubes and electrodes than I could count. They also told me I had a lung infection. I was given antibiotics for the infection in liquid form through a cannula.

So I had a new visitor. I decided her name was Clodagh Klott. I imagined her to hail from a boring mid European country which she represented at the 2003 Eurovision Song Contest. She did not fare well, but she did much better than the UK in this famous year of the nil point. I wondered if I could form a new girl band with Dolores, Peggy and Clodagh. I would enter them in the next series of Britain's Got Talent. I thought they would be different because they were all past their sell by dates. In the past I had been told to visualise the cancer now I had something else to visualise, would I be able to cope? Life was getting complicated.

I was happy to blame the flight home from Florida for the blood clot. I was convinced the journey had not done me any good. It had started badly when we arrived at Jacksonville airport because the plane to Charlotte, where we would connect with the flight to London was delayed and we could not get away from President Trump's inauguration which was blaring at us from every corner on every television screen. We mooched around looking for things to do. I had one of the best hamburgers I had ever had for lunch but we could not stretch it out any longer and so went and sat near the departure gate. It got later and later and I was sure we would miss our connection. Nothing was going right and the harsh air conditioning was making me cold and the chill was starting to make me shiver. We saw our plane land and the agitated passengers started to form a queue even though the flight was not called. When we went to board the lady checking the boarding passes told me off.

'Wearing that neck brace sir, you should have been priority.'

But judging the mood of the other passengers I think I would have sparked a riot. We did make the flight to London but not until we rushed from one terminal to another. We were amongst the last to board and the most stressed and exhausted. We had good seats by the window on our own and after calming down and our meal we both managed to sleep.

Over time and with lots of help from the staff I became more stable and was moved to one of the nursing wards where I was told I would stay overnight. I actually stayed a week. To help clear up the lung infection I was given more antibiotics. I was scared because of the fit I had had in emergency the day before. A nurse arrived with the said concoction. I warned her I might have an allergic reaction. She disappeared and came back armed for the job with various drugs which she would use to save me if I went into a fit. The nurse and the ward sister decided I should be fully hydrated in order to minimise any risks. I was put on a saline drip. More tubes for me to contend with.

After thirty minutes the concoction that was scaring the hell out of me was administered. I was told all should be okay if the saline had worked and if the antibiotics were pushed into me slowly, but to cover all eventualities antidote drugs were ready if needed. Everything was prepared except me. I did not want to go deaf, pass out, wake up with a blotchy rash or have trouble seeing my nurse. I did not want the ward to go all wobbly. Nothing happened, except I broke out in a cold sweat worrying my poor old brain might melt inside my skull again. I felt a bit of pain because my poor old veins were beginning to wear out and my nurse had trouble getting the antibiotics into me. I felt a fraud when I did not have a fit and apologised. But the nurse said it was better to be prepared. My nurse stayed with me for ten minutes in case anything did happen. Would I worry each time the antibiotics were fed to me through the cannula? Yes of course I would. By Thursday my lovely team told me they were happy for me to have the antibiotics in tablet form so no more risk of a brain melt, which we now thought was more likely to have been caused by the iodine used in the CT scan.

On Monday, Tuesday and Wednesday I felt so lousy I did not want to see anybody. I told John I could not cope with visitors.

When I was sent for an ultrasound to see what may have caused the blood clot I was not sure what would happen. I was asked to sit on a table with my legs dangling over the edge so the radiologist could move the head of the ultrasound machine up and down each leg. This lady, like other people I met in the medical profession was obviously a member of the association of slow torturers because the procedure hurt me. As she moved the machine up and the front and back of my legs she had to press as hard as she could.

'Are you alright?' she asked. 'Can I carry on? Does it hurt?'

'Yes and yes,' I told her. 'But it hurts like hell. Please carry on. I'll be okay for a few more minutes. Have you ever had this done to you?'

'No thankfully. But I do know it can be horrible and it is uncomfortable. Some guys hate it, especially if they have muscly hairy legs.' I was told lying in bed back in October may have been responsible for the blood clot, but I was sure the stress of the flight back to London was to blame.

I hated the orange pyjamas I was given to wear. Orange is such a difficult colour for anybody to carry off. They were a bit big as well and suddenly I looked like I had developed a set of man boobs. John thought I looked like an escaped convict. I thought that with the addition of a blue hairnet I could easily get a job working in a biscuit factory as a quality controller. I imagined how the look might have inspired Victoria Wood to create a character for one of her monologues. I fancied the character would ride an old bike and wear wellington boots one size too big and a knitted bobble hat. She would often talk about going to Tenerife for a holiday in the sun, but of course she would never actually make it. She would go on about her monosyllabic boyfriend who once bought her a cider and a packet of salt and vinegar crisps on a date to a village pub somewhere in Shropshire, who then stole a kiss on the way home.

My few days on the ward proved to be quite educational. I was surrounded by old men with acute problems. They had illnesses like pneumonia and other lung disorders. And boy did they make a fuss. One particular man was simply horrible. He shouted at anybody wearing any kind of uniform. He told cleaners to plump up his pillows. He never asked nicely. He barked his instructions and words like please and thank you were not part of his vocabulary. His poor wife suffered the most. He barked at her and when she asked him questions he whined on to her about not being stupid.

On most occasions he would sleep when she visited him, but he was always awake with his moaning when she was not there. She was so loyal and attentive. She went out of her way to do things for him and he rewarded her with barks and insults. I imagined him being married to my sister. Had he treated her half as badly, she would have made sure he was severely punished. I sat in my bed and pondered why some partners, both male and female put up with such abuse and still remain calm and loyal. One afternoon I awoke from a lovely warm doze, to see the old misery guts staring at me.

'Don't you give me the evil eye you old bastard,' I said loudly enough for him to hear. He sniffed and turned his head away quickly. He never looked in my direction again. The pleasure I got was enormous. I was so pleased to put this horrible, snivelling bully in his place. I did not do this for me; I did it for his long suffering wife, who sadly would never actually know what I had done for her.

The best time was when he moaned for a whole afternoon to his long suffering wife about how the doctors were doing nothing for him. He said he would never get better because the hospital was useless. The very next day a series of tests and an MRI scan had been organised for him, but when the time came he refused to go. A porter turned up with a wheelchair to take him off for his first test but he refused to get in and said he wanted to be taken for his tests in the bed. Then he refused to go at all. It was obvious he was scared. Over an hour later and after lots of coaxing by doctors he went to his first test in the wheelchair. He had wasted peoples' time. He had been rude. He had accused the staff of not trying to make him better. But during all this time the nurses and doctors had stayed polite and remained calm. When he came back from the tests he crowed to his wife how brave he had been.

This vile human being was acting just as he had done when a toddler. He was the centre of his universe and his wife just kept reinforcing that position and telling him it was just fine to behave and carry on like this. With every word she rewarded his appalling behaviour and like Mary Shelley had managed to create a monster, but perhaps not so good looking.

Another old man in the bed next to mine moaned all the time as well. But he had a gentlemanly presence and so could be forgiven. One morning he asked the nurse on duty if he was going to get better.

'Of course you are. We work miracles in here,' the nurse assured him. 'Hang on a minute. How old are you?' the nurse asked.

'Seventy four,' he replied.

'Oh dear,' the nurse said. 'The medicines we're giving you don't work on people over 60.' With this she roared with laughter and I laughed as well. The elderly gentleman must have looked shocked.

'I'm only joking lovey,' she added. 'I thought the joke would cheer you up,' and off she went humming and giggling as she did a little jig. I laughed as well, but at the same time I was a bit shocked a nurse would joke like that. The ward was proving to be entertaining.

There were only four beds in this small ward and I had two moaners and an empty bed opposite me. By Thursday the two moaners were moved. We were in this space near the nurse's station so we could be observed all the time. The two moaners were obviously on the mend despite the efforts of the staff to stop them getting better. My new neighbours were much more deserving cases. They seemed much more poorly.

I did not make friends with any of the patients. I learnt it is difficult to make friends in hospital. This may be because patients only want to concentrate on getting better, or perhaps it's because wards are such public places they will do everything they can to protect their privacy by keeping themselves to themselves, or perhaps the English are just not naturally friendly.

The ward was on the fourth floor and I was next to the window which had a great view of the Euston Road and the Euston Road tunnel. I enjoyed standing by the window looking at the traffic at different times of the day. It was interesting to observe how busy it could be sometimes and how it all slowed down as the day grew old. During my short stay I saw the road in bright sunshine, darkness, rain and snow. This road also holds lots of memories, which were now coming back to me. When I was still at college I walked down this part of the road one evening in the rain. I remember being fed up as I made my way to King's Cross station because at the time I thought London's streets were paved with gold, but I could not find any. At the time I saw myself as a bit of a failure and was getting disappointed with my lot, so I gave myself a good talking too. I remembered actually walking past Euston station getting soaking wet and talking out loud.

'Now stop it,' I told myself in a bossy exaggerated voice. 'You can buck up your ideas, get out there and make something of yourself. What's wrong with you, you great big prat?' By the time I got back to the flat I shared with Meryl and Pauline I was shivering but out of my mood and again focussed on finding that gold.

The view also took in an office building, which I had often gone to for meetings over the years. In some of those meeting rooms I had won policy battles and had enjoyed the privilege of developing new and interesting ideas.

One of the next door buildings houses the Wellcome Foundation where I went for an interview once for the best job I ever had. To get the job I had four interviews with different people I would work for or with. One of the interviews was with a director of Wellcome who could only see me early one morning and I met him in his office, where we had breakfast together with two of his policy managers. It was such a lovely way to have an interview and meet the chairman of the committee that would steer and advise my work.

By Thursday all the tubes had been removed. I was still on

oxygen and my heart rate was still being monitored, so I remained attached to the bleeping machine. But I could disconnect the monitor and take off the oxygen when going to the loo. I felt so much better. While I was in the toilet John arrived and he sat down to wait for me. When I came back from the toilet I put on the oxygen, sat down and picked up the two electrical leads to reconnect the bleeping machine. As I pushed the connectors together I asked John if I was going to be okay and then jumped around pretending to have been electrocuted. Still sitting John pushed away from me in his chair. I laughed so loud even the poor patient in the opposite bed smiled. I thought it was hilarious.

'That was not funny; you could have given me a heart attack,' John shouted to scold me. 'You could have killed me.'

'You're in the right place if you're going to have a heart attack,' I answered still laughing. He tried not to laugh but he failed when he broke into a smile which turned into laughter. Hospitals have different moods but they are never dull. The joke reminded us of a story about John's father Pat. When he retired Pat applied for a part time job as caretaker of the local primary school. They were innocent times. During the interview, Pat was asked what he knew about electricity.

'I know enough about it not to go near it,' he replied in his soft Kerry brogue after giving the question careful thought. What a wonderful answer to a stupid question. I would have given him the job. Pat was wise enough to call in a qualified electrician. A fool would have tampered where he should not tamper.

It was such a relief being able to breathe normally again. The pain had gone and I felt one hundred percent better and I had three visitors. My day was full. I looked forward to being discharged on Friday.

Going home was such a pleasure. John had made the flat look great again. It was clean, warm and welcoming; lovely. But there was a downside because I had to administer my own medicines including the blood thinner which had to be injected straight into my stomach using a hypodermic needle. I never got used to doing this and for the next five months would dread my early mornings when I would take a needle from its box and push it into my lower belly. I was still very thin and making a roll of flesh which I could use was near impossible. Disgusting.

I thought the blood clot would seriously delay my operation with Mr Choi because I did not think he would be able to operate on such a huge scale if my blood had been thinned. But this was not the case and Mr Choi was monitoring my progress. The doctor looking after me said she had never known a consultant ask to be kept informed so much. Mr Choi's office rang every day for an update. All I needed now was my call from the same office.

9. Jobs

*'I will always choose a lazy person to do a difficult job because
he will find an easy way to do it'*

Ziad K. Adbelnour

We had returned to London from Florida for my operation that had not happened to get rid of Dolores once and for all and I had run into Clodagh Klott, but how long would I have to wait for the next big operation which Clodagh had delayed?

We did not wait long. We got the call to tell me the arrangements Mr Choi and Michelle had made. I would go into the National on Tuesday February 21st and to help Mr Choi make his final decision I would have an MRI scan on Monday February 13th and blood tests on the Friday. In just over two weeks it would be done. This came as a big relief because we could now start planning our lives again. We could look forward to the operation and returning to Florida. Could we even dare to start thinking about life after Dolores? John and I could get our lives back. Clodagh had knocked us off track but our locomotive was building up steam and pulling out of the station again.

The news gave me seventeen days to do what I liked. John and I were free to have fun and organise our lives. I put on my practical head and set about doing some jobs.

Using that sensible head, the first job was to update our wills. We had been putting this off because I did not want to tempt fate. Why would I need a new will; I was not going to die?

The car had not been looked after and I was worrying about it. I am not a petrol head but I do like my car and believe in looking after possessions properly, so I booked it in for a service. At the time the mechanic unblocked the drainage system because the car had been getting wet inside when it rained and he fixed the air conditioning which had stopped working. Fixing the car helped me believe in the future again, because I became determined to drive to Ireland when we got back from Florida. I even had the car washed and waxed because I would definitely be using it again.

We were beginning to feel optimistic about the future and were pleased to accept an invitation to spend a few days in the New Forest with Kevin, Lisa and their girls and Kevin's mum and dad who had rented a beautiful house for us all.

This trip proved to be a great pick me up and welcome distraction. We had not been sure if we should go, but now we had the date for the surgery there was no stopping us and it was a good excuse to give the car a good run on the M3.

I had my MRI on the Monday at the National as planned and we were free to travel to Hampshire on the Tuesday. John and I never stop talking on long journeys but afterwards I can never tell you what we talk about, we just talk. It was a beautiful sunny day that began with a sharp frost, which enjoyed a huge clear blue sky. We were doing well and I thought when the A3 turned into the M3 we would be there in no time, but I was wrong because we hit major works on the motorway and we crawled for an hour. Apart from the delay, the drive was perfect and I loved it and it was a great test to see how my neck would cope.

We had trouble finding the house. Lots of roads were closed and the house was nowhere near the village of its address. But when we found it, it was a stunning designer house. The house was stuffed with modern furniture and antiques, which helped make it surprisingly cosy. The beds were so comfortable you just did not want to get up. The others had arrived the day before and left us the best room, but to be fair you would not really mind which room you had because they were all lovely; ours was just the biggest. We almost had a wing to ourselves. The bedroom was huge and we had a separate dressing room that you walked through to reach a massive bathroom. The shower would accommodate the local parish football team and was really its own wet room. There was also a massive bath.

On the first night we lit log fires in the two reception rooms, ate a steak dinner and drank red wine. The combination of good wine, a fine dinner and log fires tired me and I dozed off on one of the large sofas and left the clearing up to the others. Getting into bed was a dream and unlike a typical night, I slept through until nine the next morning. During the night it snowed and the view from the pretty window complete with its window seat, of the gentle rolling Hampshire country side was highlighted by a light smattering of snow. Some horses dressed in green coats were standing in a field. I have never been a fan of the countryside because I like London and am a city boy at heart, but on this occasion it did not seem so bad and I put this down to the position and comfort of the house, which had seduced me. The bathroom had a huge picture window and I continued to enjoy the view from my shower as I watched the sun get stronger and change the colour of the morning sky from a wintery watery orange to vivid blue. All was well with my world.

For our first day we drove to Portsmouth. We spent time looking around some shops in an outlet centre until it rained and we ran into a café where we bought everybody a late lunch. I felt bad the lunch was so cheap because I wanted to treat my hosts more generously, but it was a gesture and although it was only sandwiches they were excellent. The café overlooked the harbour where we watched ferries come and go to France. We went for a walk around the harbour when the brief winter storm passed and the sun came out again, but it blew cold and we all agreed we had

had enough of Portsmouth. I did not wear my neck brace until we got in the car to travel back to the house and I was pleased with how well I was coping.

Kevin suggested we stop off for a drink on the way back and he remembered a smart and unusual hotel that was worth a visit. It was dusk when we arrived at this beautiful and unique hostelry. It was an old Georgian manor house set in the middle of its own part of the New Forest. The designers had really thought about how to create a decayed look, which added to its charm. It was not pristine and deliberately tatty in places. The rooms were dimly lit, the sofas were big and faded and even the wallpapers had been aged to give the rooms an authentic look.

We sat in the bar in front of a log fire and ordered gin. Old drinking glasses of all shapes and sizes stood on glass shelves strung across the windows. I pointed out to John that we had quite a few of the same glasses back in the flat. The walls were covered with the heads of ancient wild boars that looked down on us furiously. The girls were not sure they liked them. The barman was charming and judging from the bar bill I thought he could easily afford to be. The hotel only seemed to accommodate romantic couples. Apart from our two girls the lack of children and families staying at the hotel was obvious. I noticed the couples sitting on the sofas in the different rooms giggled and stroked each other a lot and they did not appear to know we were in their company. The couples were not in the first flush of youth either, so I imagined the hotel catered for people needing a discreet place to conduct illicit affairs. I wondered how many of the people I was observing might have told their wives and husbands earlier that month they would be on a training course or at a conference. We finished our drinks and left. I kept my theories about the hotel's clientele to myself.

We spent the second day of our little holiday in Bournemouth. I had forgotten how pretty Bournemouth is. After we parked the cars we had a walk on the pier and the girls spent some time in the penny arcade trying to knock down stacks of two penny coins in the roll-a-penny machines. It is amazing how addictive and challenging it can be to try to win. The satisfaction of knocking down a few two penny coins is thrilling but short lived when you just put them all back in again, but the girls loved the innocent fun of it all.

Piers are old fashioned but never out of date and even in a technological age they bring together their combination of simple, tatty and romantic pleasures. People cannot walk past a pier; they have to walk on a pier to enjoy a different vista, the sun and the smell of the sea. They allow us to return to the sea, from which we emerged all those millions of years ago, without getting wet. We bought soft whipped ice cream with a chocolate flake and walked back to the town.

We walked through the lower garden, which even in February was full of colour. And on this particular day, we were surprised to see so many people but the weather was amazing and they were out enjoying Bournemouth's micro climate. At the end of the garden walk we crossed the road and found a café where we could sit outside and eat lunch. We were shielded from the light breeze and caught in a sun trap. It was so lovely having the warm sun shine on us. I ordered pasta, which was well prepared and tasty. We chatted and the girls made friends with a dog. After lunch we split up and went off to have a look at the shops.

I was pleased to get back to the house because I thought I may have overdone the last two days. In Portsmouth I surprised myself by walking around for hours, which was something I had not been able to do since last July, but Bournemouth had not been so easy.

My aches made sure I was not able to go out for dinner on that last night, but I enjoyed a night in the house on my own and an early night in that dreamy bed. Although I did imagine the house was surrounded by burglars, goblins and monsters. I am not keen on isolated houses stuck out in the countryside, which insist on making strange and unwelcome noises. It was a good job my housemates did not stay out until the pubs closed.

The drive back to London on the Friday was easier than I had expected because of the aches in my neck the day before and we even went out with Neil and Nichola for dinner that evening. I had to be back in the afternoon to keep my appointment for my blood test. On Saturday Robert and Mark came for dinner and Mark took us out for lunch on Sunday to one of our favourite restaurants on Upper Street in Islington, where we are sure the owner picks the waiting staff for their good looks. I wondered if Mark was treating us by spending some of the money he had made illegally on the streets of Edinburgh. All these great distractions over the last few days meant I did not have to think too much about what would happen in the coming week and I was grateful for the kindness of friends. We sent flowers to Kevin's parents to say thank you for the mini holiday.

On the Monday I put my sensible head back on and did another job, where I wrote letters to my pension providers about how I wanted John to be my beneficiary if I died on the operating table. This was something I had thought hard and long about. We had done our wills, but organising the pensions had seemed a step too far. I was not going to tell John, but I needed his bank details and he had put everything away in one of his safe places before our trip to Florida, so I had to tell him what I was up to. We both laughed and joked he might now want to add ground glass as an essential ingredient to my meals. We put copies of the letters in a plastic folder with copies of our Civil Partnership Certificate and addressed envelopes.

For the rest of the day he kept breaking out into broad smiles and I should have worried when he kept taking out the letters to read them. Was he totting up his inheritance? This is what we told friends who think us wicked anyway. But in a weird way it was a relief we did it. I knew where all the information about my pensions was stored but someone else would have had to rifle through files to work out what to do. This way it was neat and tidy and nobody was going to be troubled or put out. When you are ill, facing up to things is often good for the soul. You just feel good and really grown up about doing the jobs to put your house in order. It can take courage but the feeling you get from it far outweighs the worries and is more than worth it.

10. Scared

'You never know how strong you are until being strong is the only choice you have.'

Cayla Mills

checked into the National on the same day the largest-ever study claimed pills do work with patients suffering from depression. The researchers at Oxford University, who examined one hundred and twenty thousand people in more than five hundred trials across three decades, declared anti-depressants are helpful to the ill and hope their findings will encourage GPs to prescribe drugs to more of us. As I laid in my bed that evening I wondered if I should be given some drugs to stop me worrying about what was going to happen the next day.

The afternoon was taken up with more blood tests and another MRI. I had been given a private room up on the top floor of the hospital because there was no room on the wards downstairs. The room was peaceful. It had a private bathroom and a television and a good view over Queen's Square. When John left I felt very lonely and I wondered why private patients were happy to shut themselves away and bore themselves to death. I was sure I had healed well after each operation or mishap over the last six months because I had been part of a community on each ward. I had enjoyed my observations; even the horrible spoilt man who took pleasure from being rude to his wife.

I waited for my dinner and tried to watch the television but I just kept changing channels. I gave up and turned the television off. I went to look out the window. Up this high I could see a good bit of the London skyline and picked out buildings and monuments I knew well. Centre Point loomed up just to the left and I remembered one afternoon when the fire alarm went off during a meeting. Everybody had to walk down what looked like the back stairs including a cabinet minister who took it on himself to take the lead in keeping up everyone's spirits.

From this vantage point I could also see the tops of the buildings on the other side of the square. On the top of two buildings an enterprising property developer had added a couple of duplex penthouses, which could not been seen from the square or streets below. I could see their owners walking around their hidden world. I envied these people and thought how wonderful it must be to squirrel yourself away each night to the safety and seclusion of a luxury home built on top of such a vibrant and exciting city. From their vantage point they could be completely private but only a short hop down to all the bars, cafes, restaurants and entertainment you could wish for. Even though I could not see the residents perfectly because of the distance between us, I felt guilty peering into their worlds and so pulled down the blinds.

There was a knock at the door. Oh good, perhaps the drugs had arrived to stop me worrying about the next day. It was my dinner, which as usual did not disappoint. After my meal a friendly nurse came in to check my blood pressure.

'Are all the patients up here private?' I asked.

'Yes,' the nurse answered.

'Don't they get bored up here on their own?' I wanted to know.

'Some do I suppose. They never tell me. I think these people are used to it. They don't want to be on a normal ward,' she told me in what could have been a Polish accent.

'Are any famous?'

'I don't think so,' replied the nurse who was being discreet and who did not want to gossip. I think she had her views, which she wanted to keep to herself. But the conversation broke the ice and we talked a bit longer and I was grateful for her company. She told me she was worried about Brexit and did not want to leave her life in England. She told me her husband was an electrician who had set up his own successful business and as far as she was concerned her children were English because they had been born here, but more than that they were doing well at school and had loads of friends. I listened to her story and although I was not one hundred percent sure, I told her she and her family would be fine.

'Why wouldn't we want law abiding people like you and your husband, who pay their taxes and fix people and our electrics living here in our country?' I said to reassure her. I smiled. She shrugged her shoulders. I had had a similar conversation with another nurse when Peggy Fry was fitted.

'Here's hoping; I'll be in to check on you later,' she said finally and left. She probably did come in but I did not see her, I must have been asleep.

I woke for my next big day. Mr Choi and his team came to see me to tell me what would happen. They went through the usual scary risks, but I had heard this stuff so many times it was not so scary to me anymore. It had lost its impact. Dr Katharine Hunt came to say hello and reassure me and she told me she did not ever want to see me again. What could she mean? After all Katharine is the Clinical Lead for Resuscitation. I looked at her aghast.

'What do you mean you never want to see me again? Do you want me to die or something? Crikey that's good coming from the lead for resuscitation,' I said and we both enjoyed the joke and laughed.

The first job of the day was to fit an IVC filter to catch any blood clots that might happen during the operation.

At ten o'clock I was taken down to the imaging department to have the filter fitted. I always think going for operations and tests in a bed being pushed down corridors by a porter is hilarious and I get the giggles. There is such a sense of the ridiculous about it. When ambulances are involved it gets even sillier. The filter was to be fixed into my main artery so it could catch any future blood clots. Going up through my groin the radiologist would fit this clever bit of kit. On the screen it looked like a small spider. I would still need to have the blood thinners. The filter was put in as a precaution because of my history and because I would be immobile after the operation.

I saw the filter as my own clot catcher. I have a clot catcher. I can now do my own version of Chitty, Chitty Bang, Bang featuring the clot catcher and Dolores Toomoore as Baroness Bomburst, although she would have a hissy fit because she did not get the part of Truly Scrumptious. The possibilities were endless. But there was something wrong with this idea. My filter was elegant and able to move like a ballet dancer. Not a bit like the child catcher from the movie. So I decided to call my latest visitor Phileas Philter, Phil the vein filler. I imagined him to be a retired dancer from the chorus of the Royal Ballet, who had had an interesting and fulfilled life. He was very smart and always elegantly dressed. He could be seen frequenting the smart bars of Covent Garden, Fitzrovia and Soho. He had a wide circle of friends who he amused with his name dropping stories. One name he particularly liked to drop was Sir Robert Helpmann, who actually played the Child Catcher in the film Chitty, Chitty, Bang, Bang, whom he had met in his younger years as a new dancer at Covent Garden. He had liked the life of a dancer, but he enjoyed his retirement more.

Putting in the clot catcher is quite straight forward, but it was an unpleasant and uncomfortable experience. The pressure on my groin and the strange internal feelings caused my toes to curl. All I had put up with so far and this I hated the most; oh yes, except perhaps for the MRIs, the painful biopsy, the hallucinations, the removal of phlegm using the drowning tube and do not forget the mask fitting of course. Then there was the blood clot and the panic of not being able to breathe properly. I will have to make a list of all that happened to me so I can decide which one I hated the most, which gave me the greatest pain and which one was the funniest.

For the first time I was scared about what I was going through. I was worried about the procedure and the huge imminent operation. I had this awful feeling I may die this time. Would I wake up from the anaesthetic? There was no good reason for me to think the worst might happen, but I wondered if I was pushing my luck too far this time. If I did have nine lives, how many had I already used? I thought about all those scans, procedures and operations.

I was strangely pleased I had updated my will and written letters to my pension providers. I seemed organised and best prepared for the worst. I was smug because my affairs were in order. Had I grown up at last? I was not scared of dying mainly because I had had such a great life and if it had to end I was grateful for the life I had been given. It would have been churlish to complain. My parents had not been rich and I had grown up in relative poverty where my parents had to work hard and we lived in a council house. But my parents were great providers and my mother could run a house and make the most of the funds she had.

One afternoon when I was at college I went to see a cousin who worked at the Daily Express on Fleet Street. As I walked into the building I met my auntie Beatty who had just finished lunch with her husband who was a journalist. Back in the fifties there were lots of strong women in my life who were not actually Aunties but we called them Auntie out of respect and because they were great friends of the family. Beattie was one of those ladies.

'Jimmy,' she shouted. I hated being called Jimmy. 'How are you? Don't tell me, you look gorgeous.' She gave me one of her huge hugs. 'You got your father's looks thank God. How's your mother? What a woman? No one can run a house like your mother. Such a budgeter. Everyone says so. Give your mother a kiss for me. Must rush, I'm meeting my sister. Bye, bye my darling.' It was official, my mother was good with money. We all adored Beattie. She was glamorous, loud and always rushing and a caricature of what a successful East End Jewish lady should be like. You never had a conversation with Beattie or her sister because they always answered all their own questions; the best you could do was shake your head.

My parents had shielded me from the truth. I thought we were rich because I had no benchmark. It was not until I left home, went to college and started mixing with kids from other backgrounds that I understood where we stood in the great social project that is Great Britain. Building my life with John had provided me with all the fun and happiness I would need and being adopted by his huge family had given my life purpose. Unlike lots of people I knew my life was whole and it was free from fractures.

I had no reason to fear the actual act of death either because what I witnessed in the past was not horrible. Both my parents had in the end welcomed death. They had not wanted any more bits to fall off and had been ready to go. My mother had had a heart condition in her old age, which stopped her living colourfully. She was revived on three separate occasions. I was sitting with her in hospital the third time when she opened her eyes.

'Oh no Jimmy, not again,' mum always called me Jimmy when she was annoyed with me. I hate being called Jimmy. 'Please don't let them revive me next time. I've had enough and I'm ready to go. Do you promise?' She died on a Saturday morning. My mother had quite a few wrinkles on her face. When I went to see her after she died all the wrinkles were gone along it seemed with the pain.

My father told me nine months after my mum's death that he was also ready. He said getting to be 86 was not that great. He got his wish.

John and I were both sitting with other friends when they died and on each occasion they went peacefully. One friend died in hospital and one died in a hospice surrounded by her family. We are convinced our friend who died in the hospice waited for us to arrive. We had been told she would die quickly but we had a long drive to get to her and we got caught in slow traffic and a traffic jam on the M2. When we walked into her room she died a little later. The actual moment of death has to me always been beautiful. I have never really experienced sorrow; even my peers who died before I was twenty one were killed in accidents enjoying what they did. Dying must be one of the most difficult things we have to do. It is not easy to die.

After Phileas Philter was fitted, I was wheeled to the recovery room to wait for my big operation. I thought I had three hours to lay and think about the worst, but there were so many distractions I did not really have time to worry. Nurses made sure I was comfortable. Katharine came to see me and of course she brightened my day and two anaesthetists came to introduce themselves. One I had met before back in October.

In a quiet moment I was left briefly alone and went back to thinking I might be scared. I started to enjoy tormenting myself by telling scary stories. After a while I stopped worrying about the operation and decided the fear was mine to manage. I now knew lying in my bed that fear came from the scary stories I was telling. These stories we tell ourselves are rarely rational and we allow our emotions and imagination to distort and change what we know to be true and realistic. Being strong about what was happening was actually my best choice.

At two o'clock I was wheeled into the operating theatre. The nerves were kicking in a bit because of all that thinking about death, but by twenty past two I was off playing with the little folk. Hope they are kind fairies and not evil goblins. Falling into an induced sleep is almost magical, so perhaps good fairies really are involved.

I woke. I had not died. Wow, I could see people, walls and machines. I could hear noise. I was alive. Nurses asked me questions. I could answer them so I was probably okay. I was not paralysed anywhere. I had not had a stroke. I was in intensive care being looked after by two angels. It was nine-thirty on Thursday morning. I took some time to fully come round, but I did know I was doing okay.

Katharine came and told me what had happened. The operation had lasted six hours. I had lost two litres of blood. Katharine had stopped the operation at one point when my blood pressure dropped dangerously low. Katharine's skills had saved me again. It was not clear what had caused this blip. I could be allergic to an antibiotic or a piece of Clodagh might have broken away.

'Why do I have so much trouble with those bloody women in my life?' I asked Katharine.

'They give us plenty of trouble as well you know,' was her witty reply.

Katharine had sent off a blood sample to determine what had happened, but it would take three weeks before more would be known. Because of the blip, Katharine had kept me asleep until just now. She had decided not to wake me after the operation because my body needed time to rest after the trauma of the surgery and the blip.

As I became more aware I could see I was hooked up to several machines. My blood pressure was being taken every few minutes. I had tubes everywhere and cannulas were sticking out of my hands, arms and feet. I had a tube down my throat. Monitors were stuck to my head and chest. I had a catheter. I dozed. John and Lisa came in to see me. They were surprised how well I looked. I did not have white hands this time and they could not believe my colour as I had lost so much blood. I felt great. No pain but was this down to the painkillers or had the causes of the pain gone? Mr Choi had also cut out the large lump on my neck which had been causing me stress. Over the last few months it had grown quite a bit. Now it was gone. A new colleague of Mr Choi called Dr Russo, who is not to be confused with the Mr Russo who I first met seven months earlier, told me everything had gone as planned and the team were pleased with how it had all panned out. I would have an MRI to confirm how successful the operation had been. Dr Russo also told me that during the operation a lot had come away in one lump, including the mound of scar tissue, the tumour and some muscle. It would all be tested, but it had gone and with it the pain, which for me was more important.

My new Dr Russo asked me to work hard over the next few days to get better. At the moment I could not even stand up or talk easily. But I was determined to heal. I had healed well before and this time I decided would be no different. The tube was taken out of my throat. It was of course a bit sore but this meant that by mid-afternoon I was ready to move out of intensive care and into the high dependency unit, where I sat on the edge of the bed and put my feet on the floor. Things were looking good.

During the afternoon different tubes were taken away and cannulas removed. I slept really well. I had expected to have bad dreams like before. I wondered who would be trying to kill me this time and if I would be on the train to Edinburgh. On Friday morning one of my angels came through from ICU to check how I was getting on. The care in the National is really impressive. I even enjoyed a well prepared lunch and ordered lasagna for supper. John and Siobhan came to visit and they were both taken aback over how I had progressed in just twenty four hours since the operation. Siobhan left when I was called for an MRI, which turned out to be a bit of a palaver.

A nurse had to disconnect me from all sorts of equipment, which I had to take with me. Again my bed ended up looking like a rag and bone yard covered in items from TV monitors to oxygen tanks. Then off I went on my rag and bone bed. We bumped our way to the imaging department. The corridors and lifts were not designed for my Rolls Royce of a bed. In the MRI unit I had to be disconnected from all my equipment and transferred from my bed onto their version which was designed not to affect the MRI machines. I had to move off my bed onto their trolley. This proved difficult because I was still weak and was draped in loads of plastic tubes. I was pushed into the scanner. I was fitted with earplugs and a clamp to hold me still. For the first time ever in an MRI scanner I started to feel sick and claustrophobic. I took deep breaths. The MRI started. I clung to the panic button, which I prayed I would not have to use. For thirty five minutes I took deep breaths, said little prayers, thought about sunny places and counted my blessings and anything else to stop me being sick. I even started to punish myself by imagining what it would be like to vomit in an MRI machine. I decided I would probably choke to death. If it happened would they get to me in time to pull me out? Why was I putting myself through this torture?

I could not stop thinking about what might happen if my horrible situation developed any further. Perhaps in a strange way it even helped me cope with what was going on, but perhaps lunch had not been such a good idea after all.

I was pulled out of the machine. The radio therapists came in to see if I was okay and to inject the contrast dye for the next stage of the scan. They knew I felt ill but said it was nearly over. I agreed to carry on. Back I went into the throat of the devil. Strangely it got easier this time. The next ten minutes were not so bad. I even nodded off. Then to get back on my bed we had to do everything we had done earlier but in reverse. I was exhausted when we got back to HDU. I slept for a while and then in the early evening I was moved to the Bernard Stanley Ward where I would complete my recovery over the next few days.

I was put in bay two so I could be seen from the nurses' station, which is normal practise for patients who have just had major surgery. But this did not work out well. I was in a bay opposite a patient who had particular problems. I called him Mr Issues. He had to be accompanied by a nurse at all times. He sat and watched television with the volume turned up high. He chose what we had to watch, or rather endure. Mr Issues was watching snooker. I do not know if he even liked snooker. I doubt he could explain the rules. This was a knock out competition between one hundred and twenty six players who each played snooker for ten minutes.

My dinner arrived. It was not lasagne. Someone on the ward had ordered my meal thinking I had not ordered anything. It was fish and chips. I cannot tolerate batter and it gives me indigestion.

I asked for my belongings, which were locked away up on the top floor where I had stayed on Tuesday night. I asked for my belongings four times. A nursing assistant said he had told the nurse in charge. The stress was starting to build now. Belongings may not be important to hospital staff, which is understandable because they have so many priorities to juggle, but to a patient they are their link with normality. I needed my mobile phone because I had promised to tell John where and how I was. I had to cause a fuss to get my bits and bobs. Eleven o'clock arrived. I had taken my medicines. I was feeling rotten, worn out and neglected. Mr Issues was still up. All the lights were on and I was being Chinese tortured from Watford where snooker at full sound was booming across my bed. I pressed the buzzer for a nurse. The nursing assistant came over. He told me Mr Issues needed to have the lights and television on.

'All night?' I asked.

'Yes, if he needs it. He has to be entertained.'

'Well in that case please move me so I can sleep,' I requested.

'That won't be possible because we have to be able to see you from the nurses' station because you have come down from high dependency,' he told me. I demanded to see the nurse in charge. He looked like he would rather drop through a hole in the floor than pass on my request and I could feel his discomfort as he shuffled off. As it happened a nurse from HDU came to check on me and see if I was okay.

'Do I look okay?' I snarled. 'I am stressed. I'm tired. I'm ill and he scares the hell out of me,' I said pointing at Mr Issues.

'Try and sleep. We can't move you because.' I cut her off.

'Because the nurses have to be able to see me, I know. I know. I was told,' I was near to crying.

'So you know why. Please try to sleep James,' she persisted.

'Okay then, I'll tell you what? Call me a cab and I'll go home. I can't stay here. I won't stay here. You can put me in the corridor. If you won't get me a cab I'll get one myself,' I was cranky and getting cocky. Mr Issues had been threatening and he scared me because he kept getting up and walking into my space. I had a banana left over from supper, which I offered him to clear off and leave me alone, but he just grunted. I was not going to sleep in this situation, where I could not defend myself. I was very protective of my neck. We had invested a lot of time, effort and money in my neck. You only get one.

'You can't stop me from discharging myself, can you?' I asked.

'No we can't, but we would advise against it. You had major surgery and you need to be looked after,' the nurse confirmed. I felt bad because I had the utmost respect for this angel from HDU.

'Move me or call me a cab. Your choice,' was my ultimatum. She went off to discuss my request with the nurse in charge of the ward. A doctor was consulted who agreed I could be moved and he came over to talk to me with my angel from HDU, the poor nursing assistant and the nurse in charge. They were all very understanding and from the look on his face I think the nursing assistant was more relieved than me that I was now happier. At last I was put into a quiet, dimly lit and calm area. I craved sleep. It had been a stressful day on top of the others. I had toyed with the idea of dying and met Phileas Philter and Mr Issues. I was now in the business of recovering from the operation and getting better. I had to set myself targets.

This was the first time I had been disappointed with the National. I have nothing but praise for this wonderful institution. But what happened had been scary. But the staff fully redeemed themselves and as usual stepped up to the plate. The nurse from HDU and the doctor found a solution. It was not ideal because I was away from the nurse's station, but it was better than being at home, which would not have been fair to John or the hospital. I agreed to take responsibility for the move for my own peace of mind, plus I had my belongings. If nothing else I got away from the snooker. Even ardent fans must find over six hours of snooker at full blast hard work. I bet they take breaks by visiting the bars, taking bets and joking with friends. My only distraction from this hell was the adverts.

Perhaps I had had good reason to be scared about this point in my journey after all.

I spent the next four days recovering from the surgery. I had learned from my experiences in October and November that you have to heal yourself by eating properly and getting mobile. You give your body all the tools it needs to repair itself. You do not give in and just lay in bed. You control your illness by managing it as effectively as you can. You must not let the illness or how you feel control you. Once you get mobile your body starts to get stronger. Doctors, nurses, physiotherapists and dieticians are there to encourage and support you. They can advise but it is up to you to listen and take action. They can help you get better but they cannot make you better. They are highly trained health professionals who know how to help, but they cannot perform miracles. You have to take responsibility for your recovery and create your own miracles.

One night we had all settled down. The lights had been turned off and the shallow night lights gave out their warm glow. I had put myself in a comfy position ready for sleep. I was drifting. I was having the experience of total peace. Then she started.

'Paul, are you asleep? Paul, wake up. Wake up Paul. Come on Paul wake up. Paul, are you in pain? I need to know if you are in pain.' There was a pause. 'Paul. Hello Paul. Paul can you hear me? Are you asleep Paul. Are you in pain Paul?' The use of this proper noun turned the word Paul into the sound of bullets being fired from a gun. I lay in bed waiting to hear her say 'PAUL', 'PAUL'. It drove me mad.

She carried on until she got her way and woke up poor old Paul from his slumbers. Then she turned on his light. I was baffled. If he was so comfortable why did the nurse insist on waking him? Surely it would have been better to leave him alone. If he had been in terrible pain as she thought he might be, then surely he would have been awake anyway. Besides we had all been given our pain killers before lights out. It took me ages to fall asleep.

The guy in the bed next to me kept me amused with his conversations I overheard. One day he had a meeting with a social worker who needed to make sure he had all the resources at home so he could be discharged on Monday as planned.

'I'd be much better at home. Much better,' he said.

'Why do you think that?' the social worker asked.

'I've got lots of things to do. I'd be busy.'

'Really, what would you do at home?'

'Dogging,' he said loudly.

'That's nice. What does that involve then?' she asked. The guy's visitor came to the rescue and explained how he now says what he likes, when he likes. The family are always saying how the doctors took away his filter. Pity I thought, when they take it out, he can have mine.

Alan, Justin and Nichola came to see me on Saturday. They came in rather gingerly; quietly. They had no idea how I would look. I think they were expecting to see that big blue head. But it was not there. Even so Nichola squealed when we talked about the surgery. Justin and I played on it. Justin loves hearing about the gory bits. We talked about how good the care is and how staff from each ward came to see me in the next ward I had been moved to. Justin said that was because I had been in ICU, then HDU and now HMU – the High Maintenance Unit. He just wondered if the staff knew I was high maintenance and what they were letting themselves in for. We had a great afternoon mucking about.

As I got stronger over the four days I became more confident the pain had gone. I did have pain from the surgery and I was taking medication for that, but I was sure the pains caused by the tumour and the ugly lumpy scar tissue were gone. This was the best feeling ever. To be without pain after two years was fantastic. I knew I still had some aches caused by my body adjusting to the rods holding up my skull. In addition, Mr Choi had removed quite a bit of muscle from my neck, which had left me with an attractive dent. He had done this to get to the tumour and he had stretched other muscles, so I had lots of aching muscles including one going across the right side of my chest, but if this was to be the compromise that was okay with me. I would, over the next few weeks have to stretch the muscles out to make them more malleable and comfortable. They were my elastic bands which had tightened and curled up.

I did not have any bad dreams this time. But I did have a couple of weird experiences where I dreamt in fabulous colours. One night I dreamt the ward had been completely refurbished. It was right real posh. The ceiling matched the floor. They were a mirror image of each other. The designer had used marquetry to create a 1930s look using teak, maple and mahogany. The curtain rails were also made from teak. Along with hidden lighting the ward was a warm caramel colour. When I woke and opened my eyes I was looking at what I had dreamt. The ward was still beautiful, almost elegant. I lay in the bed thinking what a lovely place this was to recover and then slowly the ward returned to its municipal metal and plastic, grey and blue.

One afternoon I was reading a newspaper. The ward was warm and I started to lose concentration. As I began to doze a little bit of the black and white print started to move and the letters changed to beautiful vivid colours of bright blue, purple, red and yellow. I stopped dozing and woke myself up, but the print still carried on changing colours; weird. Perhaps it was the pain killers. I was disappointed when it all stopped and the print returned to black and white.

Wednesday came and I was due to go home. My nurse took off my dressing which I was dreading, so he could take out the metal clips holding my wound together. He was amazed how well I had healed and I was shocked at the size of the clips, which looked like staples. I packed up what little stuff I had and waited to be discharged. How long this time? Leaving hospital is never a swift process. The pharmacists have to prepare the drugs and discharge papers have to be written. I sat waiting for hours. I felt like Mrs Snow.

Mrs Snow is a family story, which goes back over forty years. My mother's mother ended her days in a residential home. One dark and cold November evening my father and I paid her a visit. When we arrived Mrs Snow was sitting in the entrance, which was a glass conservatory. Mrs Snow was perfect. She was very old, a little eccentric and her full head of white hair sitting smartly on top of her head just fitted so well with her name. People were fond of Mrs Snow. She was wearing a hat and coat, walking shoes and she had a large handbag sitting on her knees.

'Hello Mrs Snow; off somewhere nice?' my father asked her.

'No, I'm waiting for him up there,' she replied pointing up at the sky. 'You know, God. He's forgotten me; lost my papers. If I sit here under the glass roof long enough he is bound to see me. I want to jog his memory a bit,' this lovely little old lady explained. We laughed and bid her farewell. Mrs Snow died peacefully in her bed that night.

I eventually left at four. I sent my friends another email:

Dear Friends

I'm home. I had the operation last Wednesday. I've been in intensive care, the high dependency unit and on a surgical ward.

The surgery was a major one again but Mr Choi removed the tumour Dr Rotondo in Jacksonville was worried about. This means Dr Rotondo can turn up the dosage of proton beam to a level that will destroy the remaining cells. I have no pain and good head movement, which is wonderful. I had been in pain for two years, so the journey back here was well worth it. Mr Choi was also able to cut out a lump which has grown on my neck since Christmas. He thinks it was scar tissue from the other operations, but whatever it was it had been really painful. I still have a few aches where my body is growing to accept the scaffolding in the back of my neck, but I can cope with that.

Dr Rotondo is already using the scans from my operation to plan my proton beam treatment and Mr Choi wants me back in Florida in the next two weeks. Everyone has again been incredible.

Hope all is well with you.

Love James

11. Leaks

'Stress is the trash of modern life – we all generate it but if you don't dispose of it properly, it will pile up and overtake your life.'

Danzy Pace

I had only been out of hospital three days when Mark from UCLH rang on Friday to warn me we might be leaving a week on Sunday if Florida was ready. So Mark's phone call kick started our next adventure. I thought it would be some time before I would go back to Florida because I would need time to heal but Mark rang again on Tuesday to say we would be leaving on the Sunday as he had anticipated. We now had to organise the travel insurance and order medicines from our doctors.

I phoned the insurance company immediately. My contact was out of the office. I sent an email to my GP to request a prescription for three months' supply of those horrible blood thinners, which I used to stab myself in the tummy. He phoned me to discuss this. We agreed I would go into the surgery on Wednesday morning.

My contact from the insurance company rang back. I assumed I would have to pay an admin fee to reinstate the existing policy plus a bit more to cover any additional days, but how naïve was I? The lady at the end of the phone told me I would need a new policy. I asked for a refund on the old policy because we had only used a few days when it was bought to cover over ninety days. She told me this was not possible because by going to Florida we had started the original policy, which meant it could not be terminated and so a refund was not within the rules. I was flabbergasted. She started the long interview to determine what sort of new policy I would now need. As I answered her questions I pictured an old miser at the end of the phone, hunched over her desk dressed in a baggy old cardigan and banging on a huge calculator to work out how much money she could screw out of me. She was not working out the best policy for us. I told her about the blood clot and the premium doubled. I was even more flabbergasted. She must have been doing a gleeful dance around her desk with her baggy stockings hanging round her ankles. Then to top it all off, my miser confirmed the policy would not cover me for the cancer or any future blood clots; so the outrageous charges made no sense at all. I rang Mark for approval to go ahead. Mark's contact that would need to give approval for the insurance was not in his office. Nothing was working out and I was starting to feel the stress.

On Wednesday I went to my doctor as agreed and a nurse took a blood sample and removed the dressing on my neck. She told me the wound was very neat and clean. I collected the prescription for the blood thinners from reception. I dropped it off at the chemist who said my needles would have to be ordered. I explained I must have them in time for my return to Florida and the lady agreed to ring me when they came in.

Mark rang to say go ahead and order the travel insurance. A couple of jobs were done. The tickets came through, but I could not book seats for the first long flight to Charlotte and the computer would not connect to my printer. My stress levels were on the rise.

I did not sleep well, which I put down to worrying about the cost of the insurance and if the blood thinners would arrive in time.

I got up and went to make a cup of tea when the phone rang. I looked up at the clock on the wall; it was ten past nine in the morning.

'Hello James, this is Dr Russo. You need to be at UCLH by ten o'clock to have the filter removed,' he told me.

'Ten o'clock?' I asked.

'Yes, you must be there. You cannot travel to Florida with the filter.'

'I'll try but it will be a bit of a rush, I've only just got up.' He told me to hang up and I rushed into the bathroom. I did the lightest and quickest wash I had ever done. John got me my clothes but he was not able to come with me because as coincidence would have it he had to be at the eye hospital later for one of his eye injections to hold back his macular degeneration. I thought having an injection in the eye must be one of the worst medical procedures ever. I could not imagine having an injection in and through the eye. It was too yukky to think about. I rushed. I ordered an Uber. I got there at nine fifty and prayed I would not need to have my blood pressure taken. I was sure the procedure would be cancelled if they found out my blood pressure was through the ceiling. I was told to sit and wait. I sat and waited and I waited a bit more and I did not see anybody until well after eleven o'clock. All that rushing had been a waste of time and it had not done my heart rate much good either. I was interviewed by a really lovely nurse. Then about twelve I went through to the operating theatre. My radiologist who would be performing the procedure was charming. We chatted and he explained what would happen.

I sat up on the table and was asked to lie down. A rubber tent was arranged over my head to reduce any infections. The rubber tent smelt like the horrible old glue we used to use at primary school, which we believed was made from boiled horse bones. The procedure began and what a day I was about to have.

After a couple of minutes I collapsed. I was so ill I really thought the Grim Reaper must be sitting on the table keeping me company. I had had an allergic reaction to one of the drugs, the glue or the small amount of contrast used in the procedure. No one could be sure. Three specialist nurses and two doctors rushed in to sort me out. It took ages to get my breathing under control and I had a terrible red rash from my head to my toes. The radiologist did get the filter out and so Phileas' vacation was over; it was time for him to go home. The radiologist showed me Phileas. I was right; he was elegant and knew how to move. He looked a bit like an old fashioned champagne twizzle stick.

I spent the afternoon in recovery where I kept drifting in and out of sleep. One of the specialist nurses came to see me. The radiologist visited me several times to see how I was doing. The doctors warned me I might have to stay in overnight. They were also concerned I was on my own. By four in the afternoon they agreed I could leave. I rang the chemist three times. I was worrying again about not having the blood thinners in time. Then the chemist answered my fourth call. The chemists confirmed the thinners had not arrived but they assured me they would be in the branch the next day. Could I rely on them? What if they did not arrive? Would I be able to return to Florida? The week was turning out to be more stressful than any I had experienced before. I bid farewell to the nurses and thanked them for all they had done. An ambulance took me home and I sent out an update to my friends:

Dear Friends

Just to let you know we are going back to Florida on Sunday so I can have the proton beam therapy. Mr Choi wanted me out there as quickly as possible. But this is really quick! We have had three hectic days getting it sorted - insurance, medicines from the doctor, answering emails from America etc. Phew - knackered! On top of this John had an injection in the eye yesterday for his Macular Degeneration.

I got a call yesterday at 9.10 to go to the hospital to have the IVC filter removed. I got there in a rush and ended up waiting anyway. The appointment was for 11 but nobody told me. What a palaver. Plus the receptionist did not book me in properly so confusion reigned.

What a day? I collapsed during the procedure. I was so ill. I really thought the Grim Reaper was sitting on my bed. Three specialist nurses and two doctors rushed in to sort me out. They were marvellous. It took ages to get my breathing under control and I had a terrible rash. SCARY! I did not stop shaking for ages. The consultant did get the filter out, which is good. I spent the afternoon in recovery and am back to normal again now.

I'm dreading the trip - I hate long haul now. But hey ho let's do it. Off to sunnier weather and the apartment we have looks gorgeous.

Good wishes to you all.

John and James

xxx

Friday came as a bit of a relief. Could I relax now? It started well when the chemist rang to say they had my blood thinners and John got his medicines from his doctor. We now only had to pack.

On the Friday evening we went out for dinner with Anne, Lisa, Nichola and Siobhan to our favourite Chinese restaurant. When we arrived the staff made the usual fuss of us and again we had the best table in the dining room. Siobhan had never been here before and she thought the food was excellent. When the main courses arrived I reached over to get a piece of duck and as I did Siobhan caught sight of my new wound.

'Oh my god, I was not expecting that, it looks like a vagina,' Siobhan sounded shocked. 'You've got to take a look at it,' she told the others. Lisa and Anne looked but Nichola squealed and politely declined. Then came all the smart comments about when was the last time I had seen a vagina.

'Never,' I said, to join in the joke and add to the banter. 'Because when you are being born you do not leave wearing a pair of wing mirrors.'

Siobhan told me to be proud of my scars.

'Scars are great, because they mean you have been into battle and won. They are trophies from an interesting life. You need to be proud of them.'

We went back to the flat for coffee. Everyone was a bit tipsy. John went to the loo and rushed back into the sitting room.

'Go see the leak. We have a leak. Water is running into the bathroom,' John shouted. He was right water was coming in, perhaps from the flat above. I went upstairs but no one answered. I rang the emergency number who said they could not help me because I was a lessee. They can only help tenants. While I argued with the jobsworth, the girls' taxi came and they left. Anne stayed to keep us company and offer support. I urged the emergency staff to help. I told them about leaving for Florida on Sunday. They eventually agreed to send a plumber. I tried the neighbour again who opened the door and she agreed to let the plumber in. The plumber arrived. He visited the flat upstairs and reported back that her landlord was sending his own plumber. He left. Anne left. I sent John to bed. He was exhausted. I was now on my own.

An hour later I heard a plumber scraping around upstairs. The leak stopped. I ran the emergency helpline to thank them and they agreed to send an electrician to make my lights safe by disconnecting the light switch in the bathroom. He arrived at four in the morning. He did the job and left fifteen minutes later. What a relief. I rang the emergency line to thank them for all their help. Then whoosh, the water started leaking again, but far worse than before. Goodness knows what the lady's flat was like upstairs. I had been told the water was flowing over the top of her toilet. I rang the emergency number again who told me it was time to send in the big boys who would need to flush the main drainage stack, which they told me is beyond the remit and capability of a domestic plumber.

'Thank you,' I said, but I took the opportunity to have a moan. 'But this is why your policy to only help tenants does not work. You need to change this policy and help us all. If leaks do not get fixed or if the leak is too big for a domestic plumber to fix, you end up spending more money in the long run anyway. Little jobs turn into big jobs in the end that wastes money, compromise the integrity of the building and make us unsafe. We pay a bloody service charge for goodness sake. As a managing agent perhaps you should listen to the residents a bit more. I am grateful for tonight, but I had to plead with you.'

I finished my rant and went to turn off the electricity supply at the fuse box. I heard the big boys doing their bit to the main stack at about six thirty. A nice young man came to tell me it was all over and they had cleaned up the lady's flat. He took a few photos of the damage to my bathroom and hall and said arrangements would be made to redecorate the walls and ceiling. I will not be holding my breath. I went to bed exhausted at seven thirty and was sure a person with my recent medical history should not be so wound up.

I woke at eleven and rang for an electrician. The same guy came from the night before and made the lights safe again and he turned the electricity back on.

I could not believe what had happened since my operation. I had been scared by Mr Issues, been ripped off by an insurance miser, worried by the local chemist, collapsed in hospital, shared a bed with the grim reaper, flooded with dirty water and given a vagina. I wondered who upstairs was testing me in so many different ways.

The events of the week left me exhausted and I was sure the flight back to Florida, where forest fires had already destroyed 7,500 acres, would be a doddle after all the week's dramas.

12. Proton

'At my age the radiation will probably do me good.'

Sir Norman Wisdom

We left for Florida on the 50th day of Mr Trump's presidency, where instead of tweeting his views he chose to celebrate by posting pictures of his presidency so far. One softer shot showed his daughter Ivanka holding her infant son. I took this change of approach as a good omen and thought things might be looking up.

I was not looking forward to the journey and was beginning to think my long haul days were coming to an end but it was no way near as bad as I thought it was going to be. But it was an early start and we left the flat at six in the morning. Anne kindly took us to Heathrow and even put our luggage in the boot of her car.

I had not been able to book our seats before leaving because of a technical fault on the website, so we did not have the best seats. The seats were arranged across the aeroplane in a two, four, two formation. We were in the middle of the four seats, which meant we had to disturb our neighbours if we wanted to get up, but worse was to come. Every time the stewardess served something she left me out.

'Excuse me,' I called the stewardess. 'Can I have my meal please?' she did not apologise, in fact she did not say anything.

She came back and thrust my meal at me.

'Thank you. But why do you keep forgetting me?' I asked.

'I thought you looked like you should be on a diet. I thought I was doing you a favour,' she said with a sneer.

'A diet?' I said in disbelief. 'I've lost so much weight I have to run around in the shower to get wet. You should have gone to Specsavers.' The passenger next to me laughed; the stewardess did not but it broke the ice with my neighbour who now did not mind being disturbed when I needed to stretch. When the stewardess brought our late snack she left me out again.

'Only joking,' she said in a charming effort to mend fences. She gave me a huge wink. The banter between the stewardess and I reminded me of a story about a friend of a friend who is a steward with British Airways. He only likes working in first class. On one shift he was moved into economy against his will and he was not happy.

'Excuse me,' a lady asked him. 'Is this chicken organic?'

'Madam,' he replied in his grandest voice. 'You're in economy. I can't even guarantee it's chicken.'

We had to change planes in Charlotte. We had bought a bottle of gin and a bottle of whiskey in Heathrow, which over the Atlantic on the main flight had been in the cabin with us, but this would not be allowed on an internal flight in the States. We were going through security where we were asked if we had liquids, we said yes. We were sent back out to check it in. I had a carry on case into which we put the bottles. The bag could then be checked in. If I had not had the bag I do not suppose the bottles would have reached Jacksonville.

On the flight down to Jacksonville I had a window seat and all I could see were trees. Miles upon miles of what looked like man made forests because the trees were so uniform. Looking down on America from my seat I began to get scared by the sheer size of the place. I remembered feeling just as vulnerable when John and I flew to Australia. At one point in that journey I went to the loo, which had a window. I looked out and saw snow-capped mountains and nothing else. I went back to my seat where I had a nap. About two hours later I went to the loo again and the view was the same. Similar to that journey I was now feeling nervous. I was having trouble getting my head around how big America must be. To put it into perspective I decided Florida was probably about the size of the UK and Florida was just a little bit that happened to be attached to the big bit. I started to feel uneasy about the scale of the country I was going to live in for the next three months. Adjectives like big, huge, massive, vast and even immense were simply inadequate and just not big enough to describe what the jitters in my tummy were telling me about the sheer expanse of this place. The big words were useless. I would need to develop a new word by combining two words like vast and bloodcurdling to make vastcurdling, but this did not work either. I settled for petrifying, which was more in tune with how I was feeling.

We arrived in Jacksonville and were met by a driver, who did nothing to reassure me about the size of America when he told us Jacksonville is the largest city in the states by land area even though by comparison to other cities, it has a relatively small population. To torment myself further, I made a mental note to visit Google to check other facts about the size of the USA.

The inside of the apartment was a bit dated compared to the one we had in January, but it suited us better. One of the bathrooms had a walk in shower which was better for me. The apartment was in an up market complex, which had a beautiful clubhouse that looked like a mansion off the set of Gone With the Wind and it included an outside pool, outdoor fireplace which overlooked an ornamental lake, a basketball court, well equipped gym, library, billiards room, a private cinema and two sitting rooms where one served complimentary drinks and snacks. The apartment itself had two bedrooms, two bathrooms and those fabulous walk in closets.

A number of English families who were having proton beam therapy at the University of Florida were staying in the complex and it was great to hear their stories. I was amazed how brave and resourceful people can be. They were resigned to getting the job done and we all agreed it was such a privilege to be on the programme.

On Tuesday morning I had all my meetings with the nurses and doctors. We had to be there early. We arrived at the hospital when it was still dark and we got ourselves a coffee and a pastry. We were both talking about what might happen when a poor looking elderly black man walked in. He was wet and his old trainers were falling to pieces. He put his plastic bag down on a chair opposite us and he went to get a coffee and a chocolate donut. He sat down and started talking.

'Hi guys. Howse ya?' He did not wait for an answer and carried on rambling away in his heavy Southern drawl. 'I have been walking for hours. Since half past four this morning. It rained on me. I had my cancer on the lung and now it's gone to my brain. I'm from Atlanta and the doctors sent me here. Look at my shoes and pants. Ruined. See the mud? I got some work yesterday cleaning a yard. I got eighty dollars so I said to myself, look here old man why not get a room. I started to come here but first I went into a church. The preacher and I talked. He went outside with me to see me off. Four guys mugged us and took my eighty dollars. I pointed out one of the muggers to the police but they ain't gonna arrest him. I've been walking ever since. All night I walked. On the corner right outside here a lady stopped her car to give me twenty dollars. She said God told her to give it to me and two young black guys jumped out a car, hit me and stole the twenty dollars.'

Up to the first mugging I was sold on his story and was about to give him some money myself. We decided our little fellow probably popped in every day for a coffee and pastry when it was still dark outside. He needs to tidy up his act if wants to get any dollars off the punters.

We were asked to go through to the consulting area. My first appointment was with a nurse who sent me over to the labs for a blood test. We had to go to another building and we could not believe how cold it was outside. We returned to the nurse in the proton centre who weighed me, measured me, took my blood pressure and assessed my blood oxygen. She was very formal and all my chat failed to soften her. I re-joined John but Michelle came right out. She was so pleased to see us and we her. We hugged each other and kissed. She told us how sorry she was that she had not seen us before we returned to London in January. We asked Michelle if what our poor little friend had told us earlier could be true. Michelle explained the hospital works with local charities to help people below certain socioeconomic levels find accommodation and transport. The only truth was our little friend was a failed conman.

We went over what would happen that morning. I would have a CT scan and I might have to have a new mask made. I told her about how I had collapsed twice in London and we discussed my possible allergies because I was a bit anxious about latex, the contrast used in scans and any drugs I might have to have. I did not know what the mask was made of, I just knew it was plastic, did it contain latex? Michelle went off to alert the radiologists about my concerns.

Dr Rotondo came to see us. He was really pleased how well I had recovered from the third operation. He put this down to me being physically strong. He said I was definitely the king of recovery. I told him I felt a lot healthier than when I was in Florida in January. I said I had struggled before and was much happier now the ugly mass of scar tissue had gone from my neck. He tested my strength and reflexes and I showed him I had dealt with the drop foot and he was impressed I could walk on both heels. He asked if he should go over the risks of proton beam therapy with us. John's face turned to panic. I knew John did not want to hear all that scary information again and so I said no. But I did ask how big the tumour had been in January. I told him how I had thought it might have been the size of a pea.

'No it was bigger than a pea, more like the size of a small grape,' Dr Rotondo told me. 'We had to deal with it because it was serious. It was protruding into your spinal cord.' John started to look concerned again. 'But thankfully the operation was a success because Mr Choi has removed the tumour so we can go ahead with your course of radiotherapy to control the remaining cells.

We have to deal with the remaining cells because if they are not managed effectively the tumour will grow again,' Dr Rotondo confirmed.

Dr Rotondo told us he was travelling to Manchester in England for a few days, where he was working with the team building the UK's first proton beam therapy centre.

Dr Rotondo assured me he was confident my allergic reactions had been caused by antibiotics and I felt less worried about having the mask fitted, so Michelle and I went off to complete the task. I changed into a hospital gown and was taken into the room with the CT scanner where I was introduced to three charming ladies who, over the next forty five minutes would manipulate and torture me. The first job was to fit a new mask. I remembered vividly what had happened in January where I was laid on the table and fitted with the sheepskin hand cuffs.

The next job was to take the CT scan. My ladies put small pieces of metallic tape along my new scar so it would show up on the scan. This took some time and my neck was getting tired. They helped me lay down. The CT scan began. Half way through they came back to put in the contrast using the cannula. I was a bit nervous. I did not want an allergic reaction. Then nothing, not even the hot feeling every radiographer I had met said I might experience. I was so relieved I relaxed and actually dozed off for a few minutes. The ladies sat me up, took off the tape and shook my hand. They would contact me again on the Friday before my first session to confirm the time of my appointment on the following Monday when my treatment would begin. It would be early April.

I went back to see Michelle, who removed the cannula and took my blood pressure. One hundred and twenty over seventy, better than people half my age apparently. This was good news as it was very low only two weeks earlier as Katharine could testify and very high when all those plumbers came into my life the other evening.

We were now free to go and pick up our car. Ruth was delighted to see us and gave us more hugs and kisses. We loved the car. Our charming lady gave us a gorgeous new shiny black SUV. It was huge and really comfortable. I could have used this vehicle to earn a few bob over the next few months by running a taxi service. It had electric doors, huge seats and could carry eight people.

The next day we returned to the hospital for an MRI scan. The radiologist was a handsome silver fox. I asked him where he got his hair cut, but not knowing Jacksonville that well I instantly forgot.

We were told about a lunch held every Wednesday for people having treatment at the centre and their families. We thought we might go but we did not really relish the idea of hanging around until twelve o'clock. But as before, the MRI took over one and half hours and we did not have to hang about waiting for the lunch to start.

We strolled back over to the centre to join in. It was held on the first floor and down a few corridors. We walked into a huge room and were shocked to see about one hundred and fifty people sitting around large round tables. I thought there might be a few people, perhaps twenty. The lunch was fabulous, tasty sandwiches made with bread I had never tasted before. During the lunch there were two presentations about how proton beam therapy is being used successfully and what to do in the local area. In between the presentations the host asked patients to talk about their experiences. Alumni patients spoke first. After the first presentation existing patients were invited to tell their stories. After the second presentation about the attractions of Jacksonville, new patients were asked to introduce themselves and tell their stories.

As a newbie I volunteered. Two people spoke before me. All the speakers had been interesting and sincere, but they had all been a bit sad. One or two had been depressing and a few got a bit emotional talking about the journey they were on with their families, but they all had something in common where they all talked about how God was helping them. I was beginning to wish I had not volunteered to tell them my story. I did not think they would like to hear what I was going to tell them. The host came over and handed me the microphone. I introduced myself.

'Good afternoon. My name is James Holyfield and I'm no relation to Evander,' which got a laugh. 'I am English and live in London. I have a Chordoma, which is a rare form of bone cancer. Well that's me introduced. Now I must introduce you to three other characters. The first is Dolores Tumour. This is my tumour's name. She pronounces her family name Toomoore. She has ambitions above her station. She was a showgirl from Las Vegas who fell on hard times, so she moved in and I'm now her landlord. When I went in for one of my operations I had to have a feeding tube fitted in my stomach, so the second person you need to meet is Peggy Fry. In February I had a blood clot. I called the clot Clodagh Klott who is a singer from one of those mid European countries that used to be ruled by Russia. So I have Dolores, Peggy and Clodagh. They have formed a new girl band. You will be able to buy their first record this summer. Don't forget, it's bound to be a hit. Goodness knows they hit me. And this person here is my partner John, who has been marvellous and my strength. I would not have got this far without him. Thanks for listening.' Everyone clapped and cheered and they had laughed through my short stand up. I had managed to cheer them up and as we left loads of people thanked me. One very imposing lady told me how much she admired my attitude and she told me how I had inspired her. I thought it would be good to get to know her, but sadly I never saw her again. I thought I had enough news to let people back home know what was happening:

Dear Friends

We are in Florida. The journey was not a as bad as I thought it might be. We did not have great seats because we were tucked in the middle of a group of four, but people on either side of us were great. The apartment is gorgeous - very comfy. The complex has a clubhouse, which looks like a mansion from 'Gone With the Wind' and it has a pool with waterfalls and a private cinema. I am beginning to wonder if I did die and go to heaven.

I have had the appointments with my doctors and an MRI that lasted one and a half hours. Dr Rotondo is amazed how well I healed after the last operation. The radiotherapy starts on April 3rd. They need this time to plan my treatment. I had to have another mask made because I lost more weight again after the surgery in London. This is a horrible experience and not for someone who is claustrophobic. The mask will help me stay still and in position during treatment sessions.

We went to a lunch on Wednesday. We were surprised to see about 150 people there made up of patients and their families. The lunch included presentations from doctors about how proton beam therapy is being used. In between these short presentations patients were invited to tell their stories. One English lady talked about her eight year old son, which was wonderful. But it got a bit depressing. The host asked if any newbies wanted to say hi. I offered, but two others got in before me. Then it was my turn. I introduced myself and then introduced them to Dolores, Peggy and Clodagh. I told them I was forming a new girl band next week. They laughed all through my story and clapped. I ended by telling them not to forget to buy the girls' new record, which would be out in the summer. It lightened the mood and the lunch ended on a cheerful note.

John has a nasty horrible old cold. Imagine an Irishman feeling under the weather on St Paddy's day? It has been really cold here since we arrived. It's the drag effect of storm Stella, which is wreaking havoc just north of here.

Hope all is well with you.

John and James

xxx

We now had over two weeks before my treatment would start and I would use this time to get stronger. We had that lovely pool where we could relax during the day and we bought loads of good food that John would prepare every evening. I also noticed some changes to my body. I had for years not been able to sleep on my left side because it made my heart pound. Since the operations this had changed and I was now able to sleep on my back and on my left and right side. My finger and toe nails were much stronger. Before the operations my nails had been much weaker and had broken easily. I was not one hundred percent sure I could put these changes down to what had happened to me medically, but what else could it be?

One morning we woke and it was a bit overcast. It had been raining. By eleven the sun had come out. It was a beautiful still day. We decided to stay by the pool and soak up the sun and atmosphere and listen to the water falling in the pool from the small water falls. To get in the mood we took the long walk to the pool past the ornamental lakes and fountains. When we arrived there were two families having something to eat. Each couple had six kids. We settled down for what we thought might be a quiet day, but we were wrong. The kids started running amuck. They jumped in the water and splashed us. They shouted at each other. As they played they got more and more excited. After about ten minutes they were out of control. Hysteria had taken grip and they screamed and screamed. The girls just screamed. They made no sense at all. The parents did nothing to calm the situation. One dad actually made it worse by throwing the kids in the pool. It became unbearable. The noise was shocking. It lasted over an hour. One family left. I saw peace on the horizon. The family that left were all boys, the hysterical girls stayed for another two hours. Every now and then hysteria would break out again and they ran about like banshees. We did not relax until they actually left the premises.

That night I did not fall asleep straight away. I laid in the dark quietly thinking about what had happened to me. I did not worry about the future and only thought about how my poor little body had been torn apart. How I had given my body over to people I did not really know. The surgery had been brutal and they had sawn and cut me, sewed me up and stapled my skin together. Who had fitted the catheters? Had Katharine fitted the tracheotomy? Did she have to push and pull? What about all the blood I had lost? Even the biopsy back in July last year had hurt me and left me weak. Getting the feeding tube in my stomach had been a challenge. I saw myself lying on the operating table being shoved around like a dead carcass. Then I rethought what must have happened. I remembered how respectful the staff had been and to what lengths they had gone to protect my modesty and maintain my dignity. I decided I could not have been treated like a carcass. My skilled and talented healers would not have allowed it. Mr Choi had used high precision tools to cut my jaw. The nearly invisible scar on my chin was proof of that. I allowed one tear to escape and as it rolled down my cheek I quietly fell asleep.

I had a dream, which I had had several times over the last six months. I was visiting a village in a pretty remote part of England. It was raining heavily. We were sheltering in a lovely old beamed pub. The publican told us we would not be able to leave the village because the three rivers that met nearby were in flood. We tried to leave but every route we tried to take was cut off by torrents of violent water. We did not get wet and we did not seem to be in any obvious danger, but we were scared and felt marooned. We would have to wait until the flood died back. The dream felt like a metaphor for what we were experiencing. We could not escape but we felt safe and we had to be patient so I could get better.

During our free time we did not bother getting up too early. One morning I got up and made a cup of tea and turned on the television to watch CBS news. I was beginning to realise the news is always about what the President is doing. I took John in his tea and his two biscuits. We sat on the bed watching reruns of the Golden Girls, which is set in Florida so we thought it was appropriate.

'We have breaking news and we are going straight to our correspondent in London for more information,' I heard the newscaster say from the other room. My good ear was obviously tuned in to pick up the word London. I jumped up and ran into the living room. 'People have been attacked outside the Palace of Westminster, which is the seat of the British Parliament. British police have not confirmed if anyone has been killed or how many people have been injured. But this is an audacious attack when you think this is right here in central London and right at the heart of government.'

We were glued to the television for the rest of the morning eager for news from our hometown and from the area where for years I had had my office and during my later years had fought battles in stuffy rooms around Westminster.

'We are told the attacker was a 52-year-old Briton,' the newscaster told us later. 'It seems he drove his car into pedestrians on the pavement along the south side of Westminster Bridge and Bridge Street. He has injured more than 50 people and five of them appear to have been killed. He then crashed his car into the perimeter fence of the Palace grounds and ran into New Palace Yard, where he murdered an unarmed police officer before he was shot by an armed police officer and died at the scene.'

Later we found out the murderer said in a final text message that he was waging jihad in revenge for Western military action in Muslim countries in the Middle East. The Amaq News Agency, which is linked to Islamic State, claimed the attacker answered the group's calls to target citizens of states that are fighting against it, though this claim was questioned by the UK police and government who found no link with a terrorist organisation and believed the murderer acted alone.

We just felt sick and sad about what was happening in the city we call home. The next day we went to the supermarket we were using. On the checkout the lady offered her sympathy as she asked me to put in my PIN.

'You're English?' she asked.

'Well I am, but John is Irish actually,' I said.

'Oh I'm so sorry about what happened in London yesterday,' she continued.

'Thank you. Actually we don't live far from where it happened and I used to work round there,' I said.

'Don't worry,' she continued. 'That nice Mr Trump will send over more troops to defend where you live in England.' She handed me my receipt and a voucher for money off my next purchases. I thanked her and left it at that. I did not want to tell her London was actually free of American soldiers. She must have thought America was helping us fight terrorists and I did not think it was my job to spoil her view of the world. I thought it was rather sweet she cared so much about me and my fellow countrymen.

'See you again next time,' I said and we left. We later observed that every time we went shopping the bill was always about one hundred dollars no matter what we purchased, which we thought was odd.

Michelle rang on Friday with some disappointing news. She apologised and explained that my treatment would start later than planned on Monday April 10th because Dr Rotondo needed more time to develop my specific treatment plan. Michelle told me Dr Rotondo is a perfectionist and he never delegates a patient to someone else. The knock on effect would mean staying in Florida for longer. We would have to change our flights and update the insurance, which judging from what happened in London the last time I contacted the insurance company would not be easy, but we agreed not to do anything until things were clearer and everything had been agreed. In addition, the hospital would be closed while we were there for two days; one for maintenance and one to observe Memorial Day, which would mean staying even longer.

The good thing about the change of date was we would be around on the Monday to pick up our two friends Neil and Nichola from the airport who would be arriving from London for a visit. But as usual this did not work out as expected. Neil and Nichola did not arrive until Tuesday. They had a terrible journey because of shocking weather. Their plane was diverted to Dallas where they had to change flights to Jacksonville, but there were no flights. And no wonder; horrendous thunderstorms had closed the airport. Back in Dallas Neil and Nichola were not given any information and they were stuck there for hours. They used Messenger to tell us what had happened and keep us up to date with what was or not happening.

It started to get late. John and I ate the dinner he had prepared and we put what was left down the waste disposal. I told them to come to the flat but they said no and told us to go to bed. They eventually left Dallas and got to Jacksonville at three in the morning after one of their worst journeys ever. They flew through a major electric storm that buffeted their aeroplane. When they arrived in Jacksonville, they checked into a hotel, which turned out to be a waste of money. They could have come to the flat anyway because we could not sleep due to the storm. There were no breaks between the lightning and the thunder and it roared for hours. The rain was torrential and Neil and Nichola had risked life and limb flying and driving through terrible weather.

Over the next three months we would experience pretty extreme weather compared to what we are used to in England. It had already been cold but a lightning storm would start a forest fire just north east of where we were staying. It would get really hot and during nearly two weeks of heavy rain the humidity would be unbearable. The weather at home by comparison seemed almost benign. In Florida we were living with an angry beast that could easily lose its temper. Our weather at home was weedy where you might get a bit wet now and then and the lightest dusting of snow would close airports. But our forests are not set on fire and trees rarely crush houses. Living in the centre of London is a bit like being in the middle of a Russian doll where I am cocooned by the flat which is in a block, which is on an estate which is in a parish, which is in a borough, which is in a city which is in little old benign England, which is part of the UK. I had swapped that feeling of safety for vastcurdling, bold America with its angry weather.

Lying in bed watching the sky light up and listening to the sort of thunder I had never heard before was scary, but at the same time strangely thrilling.

We were so relieved to see Neil and Nichola on Tuesday morning. When they came in we were all so excited we all talked at once, where each of us wanted to tell the others how worried we had been and what a terrible night we had just had. They told us the flight was bad enough but the drive from the airport to downtown Jacksonville had been the scariest because of the strength of the rain. We gave them the royal tour of the clubhouse and told them we would be staying longer than planned.

We spent the afternoon at the beach and because Neil is a regular visitor to Florida due to his job, he pointed out shops to us and told us which ones to use. That evening we went for a Chinese meal in St John's. The weather had calmed down and it was a beautiful warm sultry evening. We dressed up a bit to make the most of Neil's only evening with us. Neil had to leave early the next day to go back to his job. He had a terrible time getting a flight because of the disruption caused by the storms and ended up driving all the way over to the airport at Orlando. He had arrived late and cut short his stay with us.

While poor Neil was driving across Florida, John, Nichola and I sat in the sun by the pool. We had a lovely week with Nichola.

On the Saturday we had a super meal in an Italian restaurant where we met two friendly couples in the bar where we had beautiful gin and tonics. The dinner portions were huge and the chef came out to apologise to us because we had to wait for our starters, which were not put on the bill. We agreed this would not happen at home.

We returned to the hospital on Monday April 10th as arranged for my first treatment. The TrueBeam treatment was quite straightforward and it only took about fifteen minutes including changing into my surgical gown. I had seventeen treatments over seventeen days. TrueBeam is a form of traditional radiation treatment where a high energy photon beam is used to treat the cancer. Unlike proton beams, photon beams will damage healthy cells as they pass through the body to reach the cancer cells and other healthy cells as they leave the body. The advantage of the

TrueBeam machine is that it uses X-rays to position more accurately where the radiation needs to go. The TrueBeam machine rotates around the patient to deliver the radiation therapy from different angles. In my case I was zapped from three different angles every day.

Each day I would wait to be called and then I undressed and lay on the table. The mask was used to pin me to the pillow and I would put on my handcuffs and push myself rigid. The radiologists moved me around to line me up in the right position. When they left the room the X-ray machines rotated over me to complete the imaging. Once this was completed the Truebeam rotated over my head. Inside the mouth of the machine is a rectangular aperture made up of thin strips of metal on the left and on the right. These strips of metal move backwards and forwards until a hole is formed through which the photon beam would pass. These metal strips, known as blockers help make sure the photon beam is properly targeted at the cancer cells left behind by Dolores. After a few days I got used to the different shapes the metal strips made when they were moved. The first looked like the map of Ireland, which I thought must have been a good omen because of all my connections to the Emerald Isle. The second shape was the profile of an Egyptian goddess. The third shape reminded me of a medieval leather wine bottle.

Each day I would lay and wait for the machine to rotate. Ireland would be directly above my head. The Egyptian goddess would move to my right and the medieval leather wine bottle would move over to my left. Then it was done. I had been zapped.

Nichola left on Tuesday, the second day of my first lot of treatment. John, Nichola and I went to the hospital for a nine o'clock appointment. We were about to leave the centre but Nichola and I went off to the toilets. I came out of the gents to find Nichola waiting for me in the hall. The zip on her tight black trousers had broken. She could not take them off. I tried to release the zip. No good, it would not budge. The three of us went out to the car park where we had to cut Nichola out of her trousers. Picture this, two guys from London cutting a beautiful woman out of her clothes behind a parked car in a car park. Nichola got another pair from her case and went back into the hospital to change. Imagine if it had happened on the plane later in the day? She would not have had access to scissors or a change of trousers and might have had to walk through Immigration in her undies. More importantly, how would she have used the aeroplane's toilets?

We went into Downtown Jacksonville and had a good lunch. We sat on the pavement under a sun umbrella and ate sandwiches. The business centre of Jacksonville was prettier than we had imagined. Then we took Nichola to the airport.

On the second Wednesday after starting my treatment I had a meeting with Michelle and Dr Rotondo to review progress and monitor any side effects.

When we left the apartment to go to the hospital the air was thick and the atmosphere felt brown. The sunlight was muted and everything had taken on a dismal orange aura. The car was covered in ash from the forest fires that were raging to the north east of the city. These fires had been caused by the lightning from the recent thunder storms. The Floridians told us this was okay and we should not be worried, but to us one hundred and twenty thousand acres of burning woodland was a big deal. My jitters about the size of America and the extreme weather returned. I blessed the timid English weather and the gentleness of an April shower.

After being zapped I went to see Michelle and Dr Rotondo. I had my vitals done; blood pressure, weight and temperature and we were shown into the room with the computer. This was the same room in which Dr Rotondo had in January told me Dolores was back. We sat scared. Was I about to be given bad news again? There was a box of tissues on the round table we were sitting at. The omens did not look good. Dr Rotondo was busy and had been delayed. He came in with Michelle. We moved to the examination room. So he did not want to use the computer to show me a distressing sequel entitled 'Dolores becomes a grandmother'. He told me everything was looking good. He only asked me to maintain my weight because he had already adjusted the level of proton I would be receiving because I had gained eight pounds since my last visit to Jacksonville but this week I had already lost three pounds. I would need to keep it at about one hundred and fifty pounds. This would prove to be more challenging than I thought. I would experience nausea over the next few weeks and I lost my appetite. Even food adverts on the television made me heave. But I could not be physically sick. I had lost the mechanisms due to physical changes in my throat and the surgery on my tongue has left it shorter than it used to be. He also told me to drink plenty of water to remain hydrated but told me to lay off the alcohol.

I asked Dr Rotondo if I would have an MRI scan before leaving for London to confirm the radiotherapy treatments had been successful. Dr Rotondo told me no.

'You will have an MRI in about three months after returning to London. An MRI now would not tell us anything because of possible swelling caused by the radiotherapy. You are having radiotherapy because the operations could not safely remove the entire tumour, especially where it was. Deeper surgery may have compromised your mobility and caused some serious neurological problems. In addition, the tumour was unusually large. The radiotherapy is designed to destroy the remaining cancer cells and is organised in three stages. The final stage will concentrate on the pocket where the tumour was.'

I imagined Dr Rotondo was taking a wrecking ball to the flat where Dolores had lived rent free. So far so good and I could cope with this information, but Dr Rotondo went on. 'The big aim is to stop the tumour growing again. It is unlikely the tumour will be totally destroyed but the idea is to keep it in check.'

This was a bit of a bombshell. In the back of my head I think I had known this, but I had hoped Dolores would be destroyed; killed off completely. Talking to a fellow patient later in the month I discovered several patients had experienced the same disappointment. 'You will have regular imaging back home in order to monitor the tumour and see how it is behaving,' Dr Rotondo continued. 'Blood tests cannot monitor how a Chordoma performs. You will need regular MRI scans. The thing about radiotherapy is that everybody is different and different tumours respond to radiotherapy in different ways.' I clung to this glimmer of hope. Perhaps the proton and I would together get rid of Dolores once and for all. Time would tell.

On the way back to the apartment I had to fill the car with petrol. We hated buying petrol because every garage seemed to have a different system. Every time we bought petrol we caused havoc and had to be rescued by a kind passer-by. We had no choice but to use another garage we had not been to before. We drove onto the forecourt and up to an unsuspecting petrol pump. I got out of the car. I opened the car's petrol cap and put the nozzle in the hole. I squeezed the trigger. Nothing happened; it was obviously not working. I walked over to the shop to tell the lady.

'Excuse me I would like to buy some petrol please,' I said.

'Some what?' the lady asked.

'Petrol; I need to buy some petrol.'

'What's that?' I was a bit lost, confused. I knew I was going to sound horrible and patronising.

'The stuff that makes the car go,' I said, but I did not know what else to say.

'Oh gas, you mean gas.'

'Yes, I need gas that's what I meant. Sorry.'

'Card or cash?' she asked. I decided cash. She asked me how much and I said thirty dollars. She asked for the cash in advance so she could programme the pump to dispense the requested amount of gas. My wallet was in the car. I went back to fetch my wallet and returned with the said amount of money. Phew, perhaps I could now fill up and leave. I took the nozzle out of its cradle, pushed it into the hole and squeezed. Nothing happened. It was definitely broken. I went back in and joined the queue. We talked again:

'Sorry but the pump is broken.'

'No it isn't. Did you release the lever?' I felt her anger.

'What lever?'

'To start the gas, PETROL, you have to lift up the cradle which is the lever.'

'Oh sorry, I didn't know that,' I hissed. I went back out again. It was a hot day and I was now sweating. This time I lifted the cradle that housed the petrol pump. It worked. The gas was pumped into the car but to my horror it only took twenty five dollars and I had asked for thirty. Compared to the UK I had forgotten how cheap gas is in America. I needed my change. I reluctantly walked back into the shop. The lady knew what had happened. She stood behind her counter holding out the cash in a deliberate way, which she handed to me with a look of victory. I smiled weakly and walked away. The lady had beaten me. I was defeated.

'You make sure you have a nice day now,' the lady said through slightly clenched teeth. 'Be sure to visit us again, REAL soon.'

'I will. Thank you,' I said pathetically.

The people who managed our apartment complex organised social events to help people living there meet each other and perhaps become friends. They organised a wine tasting evening held in the clubhouse. We went along and had a lovely time meeting people. It was not well attended but it was only the second event following a party they had organised last Christmas. The small numbers did not spoil the evening and I thought I would treat myself to one glass of white wine. Naughty. When we got back to the apartment I started to feel unwell. I felt like I wanted to be sick and my head swam. The white wine came up violently and without any warning. It came down my nose and out my mouth as bubbles. I had turned an ordinary white wine into champagne. Although the experience was horrible, John and I laughed about it but I promised not to drink again, which was odd for John because when we went out for a meal he could not drink a whole bottle of wine on his own and this is how we discovered a new rule. One night we returned to the Chinese restaurant where we had gone with Neil and Nichola. The charming waiter asked us if we wanted to take any of the food we had left.

'Just the prawns please,' I told him. 'But we would also like to take the wine if that's okay. There is still half a bottle.'

'Of course sir; I'll fix that for you,' he said and he cleared the table. A little later he returned with the prawns and the wine, which he had sealed in a bag to which was attached the bill of sale.

'Why the bag?' John asked.

'It's in the bag to show you did not open the bottle sir and the receipt proves you bought it here to have with your meal. If the police stop you and it's not in a sealed bag they will think you've been drinking while driving the car,' he told us.

'Crikey,' I said. 'But if you think about it, that is a brilliant idea. It must stop all sorts of problems.'

'Yes, but I can't imagine it going down too well in Ireland,' John joked.

'Oh yes and please put it in the trunk of your car,' the waiter advised. For all his efforts, our waiter had earned a larger tip than we would usually give. It amused us how in America it is acceptable to have a gun in the glove compartment of a car but an open bottle of wine must be put in the boot in a sealed bag.

That night during the quiet time before you fall asleep and your brain goes into free fall and goes over the events of the day in colourful and madly creative ways, I summoned up a priest who preached about the evils of the demon drink. This preacher of the fire and brimstone variety was getting excited about what drink was doing to members of his congregation. After the service a young man came into the church when the preacher was counting the collection money. Thinking he might be about to be robbed he took a gun from the drawer of his desk and shot the intruder. I fell asleep.

We heard on the news the next morning how three people were

shot near St John's where we had enjoyed our Chinese dinner.

The second event at the clubhouse was a pool party, which was very well attended. A disc jockey played very loud music and ran competitions and food was prepared on the barbeque. We did not stay for this because we could not get a seat and I was a bit fragile by this time. I needed to sit down and found standing for any length of time difficult.

The third event was the best. It was another wine party with loads of cheese, grapes and crackers. We met some great people who told me about their lives. Needless to say I kept away from the pinot grigio. One lady I spoke with was a teacher who told me that in her younger days she been a bit left wing and had gone on various demonstrations. She had campaigned on all sorts of liberal issues. She told me she worked with difficult kids whom she loved but she said her history meant she had not been promoted. She blamed her lack of progress in the profession on her political views.

'I find that difficult to believe,' I told her. 'I thought America has a reputation for new ideas and social reform.'

'Perhaps it has. But listen, I'm not being a big head, but I know I am a good teacher. I work with kids who have real big problems and not just poor kids but wealthy kids as well. Parents tell me I work wonders and the kids like me, so why do I never get jobs I apply for? Why do I not get promoted? I'm on a blacklist somewhere,' she told me in a very matter of fact way devoid of any anger or emotion. I wondered if what she had told me could be true and if this also happened back home. We raised our glasses to each other and I toasted her with sparkling water.

Everywhere we went we met friendly and hospitable people. Americans are kind and always interested in the lives of other people. Some of the people we met at the hospital invited us to their homes. We got very friendly with Joyce, who baked me a banana and pecan loaf when I was going off my food, Siggy who shocked us with her bold stories about when she worked as a fashion model in Germany and Gilly who gave us souvenirs from the Kennedy Space Centre, where she and Joyce and their husbands had all worked during the exciting days of the Space Shuttles. Siggy and her husband went back to their home in Tampa every weekend and they asked us to join them, but I did not think I would be able to drive that far. I had to remind myself we were not on holiday but were here to sort out Dolores. By the time we left Florida we had contact details for a number of people and we all promised to keep in touch.

When I started the proton beam therapy we had to be at the hospital earlier than usual. We did not sleep well because we both kept wondering if the alarms on the mobile phones would wake us up on time. I went to the toilet four times. We would be exhausted in the morning. I got up before the alarms and made a cup of tea. We left the apartment at seven o'clock. The journey itself was easy because the roads were quieter than expected, except for the first bit when we left the complex. We went through the gates and there in front of us I could see a large family of Canada geese or is it a large family of Canadian geese? As we drove up to them the large proud leader jumped down off the grassy bank and started to walk across the road. I slowed down and stopped and we waited while each one slowly and deliberately waddled their way to the other side. We thought it was great the birds have precedence over cars and we had been charmed before when we saw drivers stop to allow them to pass. But today I was in a hurry and I was convinced the number of birds had doubled or even trebled. The birds made their loud honks as if to tease and rile me, so in response I shouted their real name at them through the windscreen.

'Hurry up you annoying bunch of Branta Canadesis,' I screamed because it sounded more like I was swearing at them. In spite of my efforts the birds would not be hurried and we had no choice but to sit and wait and count the rising heart beats.

It was a beautiful morning. I loved these early Floridian mornings when a light mist hung over a wide expanse of grass near where we lived. The grassed area was surrounded by ancient oak trees covered in Spanish moss. It was a view I never grew tired of but John was not so keen and he failed to see why I enjoyed it so much.

My appointment was scheduled for eight but I went in at seven fifty. My radiologists were called Robert and Dominick. Robert told me the session would take about forty five minutes today because they first had to get me set up. X-rays would be used to set up the proton beam machine. Eight brass apertures shaped like cylinders and the size of soup bowls, had different shaped holes cut into them. These would be used to make sure the proton beams were delivered exactly to where they were needed.

Robert asked me what music I wanted to hear. I told him I did not really mind. He played rock and roll songs from the fifties and sixties. I got up on the hard flat bench and I was put into my mask and handcuffs and reminded to be as still as I could. The X-rays machines came out of the back wall behind me mechanically. One stopped above my head and the other stopped by my left ear.

'One, two, three o'clock, four o'clock, rock
Five, six, seven o'clock, eight o'clock, rock
Nine, ten, eleven o'clock, twelve o'clock, rock
We're gonna rock around the clock tonight.'

I had trouble keeping still with Bill Haley blasting through the speakers. I wanted to jive or at least jiggle a bit. I laid there and counted the songs. I figured that if a song lasted about three minutes and four songs had played then twelve minutes must have passed. I knew the fifth song.

'And then he kissed me
He kissed me in a way that I had never been kissed before
He kissed me in a way that I want to be kissed forever more.'

Keep still. I had lost count of the songs when Robert came in. He wanted to move me. I was not lined up properly. I could not move my neck on my own. I would use my hands but they were in the handcuffs so my arms were constrained. Dominick and Robert shuffled me about. They left.

'Oh, when the sun beats down and melts the tar up on the
roof
And your shoes get so hot you wish your tired old feet were
fireproof'

The Drifters sounded great, but I could not drift off. The mask was pushing down on the left side of my nose and it began to hurt. I was not in the best position. My left eye started to water. Robert came back. He told me this was not working and they would have to start again. He removed the mask. I told him it hurt. He put a little sticky pad where the mask had pushed down on my nose. They fitted me back into the mask and shuffled me around. A few more shoves and I felt more comfortable. It must be better now. Robert seemed more hopeful. He left and the X-ray machine came back over my head. It must be working; please let this work.

Dr Rotondo looked at the results remotely on a computer. He was happy and so we were set. Keep still. The X-ray machine could now do its job. Robert was now able to use his eight brass apertures. This took some time and I was treated to more songs and more rock and roll. Elvis sang two songs I had never heard before. How many songs had I heard? I had lost count. I must have been there ages. I was beginning to ache. I had pins and needles in my wrists. My heels started to feel sore.

'Do the Harlem shuffle
Shake a tail feather baby
Shake a tail feather baby.'

Sorry Mr Earl Nelson and Mr Bobby Relf but I'm not allowed to move. I could not shake anything. I cannot even shuffle. I cannot move at all. I'm in pain. This is hell.

Dominick came in and said they were ready. Everything had been prepared and I was at last lined up properly. I would now be zapped four times for the first time using proton beam. This is why we had travelled over three thousand miles. What would it be like? And how much longer would it take. How many more songs?

When it was all over I could not stand up straight away. I was stiff and sore. I climbed off the table and hobbled back to the changing cubicle. I stretched and bent myself back into shape. But after I dressed I walked back to reception very slowly. John was relieved to see me but he was concerned because I was shaking. It was nearly ten o'clock. I had been strapped down on the table for just short of two hours. Crikey, I had probably listened to three CDs worth of great songs.

Michelle came looking for me. She thought I had forgotten my appointment to see her and Dr Rotondo. She explained that sometimes it does take time to set the machines up and get the patient into exactly the right position for the radiotherapy to be delivered precisely where it is needed.

We loved our Wednesday surgeries with Michelle and Dr Rotondo. Michelle works with me first to see how well I am doing and to sort out any problems. On this particular Wednesday we wanted to know more about when we might be returning home, mainly because John had appointments in London at the Western Eye Hospital for his injection for macular degeneration and he might run out of blood pressure tablets. Suddenly Michelle and John were discussing his problems. John was being fussed over. He had his blood pressure taken and he told horror stories about his past medical history.

'Well this is nice. It always goes back to John. EXCUSE me, but I'm the patient here. I'm the one with the cancer. This is MY surgery. It's always about JOHN,' I said clipping my words to give them emphasis. Enjoying the joke, the three of us started giggling. Dr Rotondo came in to roars of laughter. He only asked me to maintain my weight.

The True Beam machine had been very gentle; almost balletic. It made swooshing and swooping sounds and was elegant. The proton beam machine was the opposite. It was clunky and noisy. If the True Beam machine was like a trained ballet dancer, Master

Proton Beam was a bit of a thug.

On Friday I had my third session of proton. It was stressful. The mask hurt my nose again and it took ages to get me in the right position. Unknown to me I was left lying on the table because the computer had a blip. It went down and had to be rebooted. My nose was in pain and I called the radiologist as best I could with the mouth guard stuck in my mouth to hold the mask in place. I grunted as loud as I could. They took off the mask, cut a piece out and put on another protective sticker. It fitted better now. The mask still pushed on my nose and it was less painful but I had had enough. I had a wobbly moment and wanted to go home.

The plane landed at Heathrow just after seven on Saturday morning. It had been a rush to catch the plane the day before. When we left the hospital I made up my mind to leave. I was not going to go through all this pain every day. We were lucky to get two standby tickets. It had been a rush to get packed and the car back to the rental office, but we did it, we had escaped. Had I signed my own death warrant by returning home? Would the tumour remain stable? What would my medical team in London say? Would I be told off?

When the radiotherapists came back in I woke from my brief visit to Heathrow. I had been on the table for one hour and twenty minutes this time.

'That's it Mr Holyfield, all done,' Robert said. 'Sorry it took so long again but it will get better as we get used to what we need to do for you.' They helped me up and I would have to go and stretch myself back into shape. I had not returned to London after all. That would have been out of character and cowardly. Why would I let down all the people working hard to give me my life back? I owed it to the medical teams, John, our friends and me to see this through and I had the weekend to put the whole experience back into perspective. Besides I had so much to look forward to, such as sticking a needle into my stomach every morning.

There was a great social side to the hospital where the entertainments director organised events and trips. Every

Tuesday a lunch was organised to a local restaurant or organisation including museums and even the Federal Reserve to see the mighty dollar. The poster advertising the visit was to an Englishman bizarre. The poster told people who signed up for this trip not to wear shorts and leave their guns at home.

The social side was so good. I was talking to one of the retired gentleman patients who told me he would have to get a job when he got back home because he would miss the laughs and the company. Perhaps cancer had woken up his brain as well and new vivid memories were being created. Everyone got on so well and people made friends. I am convinced that this is an important part of the healing process. We met some smashing people who told us about their lives. We learned from them and they loved our stories of life in London. But and it was a big but, the one thing that broke my heart was to see the children. Many had brain tumours. They had lost their hair and some had had what looked like brutal surgery. To see these little people, many under the age of five with their wounds walking off bravely to be zapped never failed to move me.

One little boy was a real toughie. He threw himself around the lobby when he played. He stood his ground and was as tough as nails. I loved him. A little English girl who was always dressed in pretty frocks constantly asked questions as she walked between her parents chatting away and telling them what she thought of it all.

One day I was waiting to see Dr Rotondo and Michelle for my weekly surgery and I watched her walk down the corridor to the treatment rooms chatting away and disappear into the room where children are put to sleep in readiness for their treatments. I blubbed. John put his arm around me. Was the whole experience dulling and rubbing off my tough bits? The beauty is these really young kids will not remember what happened. Mitch told us they do not lose many children and this centre has the best success rates. I could only think about the ones who did not make it. I did not want to know the numbers.

On a tour of the facility one Saturday our guide told us the centre treated a lot of older guys with prostate cancer. He told us that what these men paid for their treatment kept the lights on and doors open. As a not for profit organisation the university uses the money to continuously carry out research to improve proton therapy, develop new techniques and provide American kids with free treatment, which I thought was just wonderful. I blubbed again. The Norwegians and the British NHS pay for their children to be treated. Fair enough.

On the fourth day of the proton treatment I lost my sense of taste. No matter what I ate it all tasted the same. John cooked me pancakes but all I could taste was dull flat bread. The pancakes had lemon and sugar poured over them. I knew what lemon should taste like. I could see the lemon on the plate, but I could not taste it. The lemon juice just had no taste. It was an odd sensation because I had not lost my sense of smell, which was weird to me because I always thought smell and taste were related and depended on each other. I put this change down to how my brain was confused after having to compute so much scary information recently. I could smell the pancakes but when I ate them I could not taste anything. You cannot live on smells, so I developed new eating strategies to maintain the weight I needed for the proton beam treatment to be successful. To help me I was prescribed fortified milk shakes similar to those Peggy Fry had helped put in my stomach last autumn.

I continued to have my weekly surgeries with Michelle and Dr Rotondo. On one occasion we were waiting to be seen when an elderly lady arrived in a wheelchair. I thought she was wearing an extravagant ruby necklace. On a closer look I saw the rubies were actually huge blisters which I assumed were burns from the treatment she was having. Her ancient thin skin was no match for the power of the radiation she was being given. My only problem was the nausea and I was given a prescription. I visited the pharmacist to get tablets for the sickness feeling and some laxatives because the tablets for the nausea would cause constipation.

'There you have it,' said Michelle. 'We give you a tablet that will make you stop and then we give one to make you go.'

We made four visits to the pharmacist before we were eventually given the tablets for the nausea on the Saturday. At the next surgery we told Michelle what had happened. Michelle was annoyed because the contract they had with the pharmacist was very valuable and the pharmacist did not have to go to the bother of claiming the money back from insurance companies. On our next visit we were treated like royalty. We wondered if they knew it was us who had shopped them. They tried so hard, but they still got my prescription for some laxatives wrong. I went back in and they promised to correct it straight away. We had to wait again while the missing medicines were dispensed. The lady called me over and apologised again. She was so sorry we had spent nearly an hour in the pharmacist.

'Well you can go now,' she said as she handed me my tablets and apologised again.

'Yes I hope so,' I giggled but I do not think she understood why I did.

I was getting used to the routine of having the proton beam treatment and I was becoming more familiar with what was involved. We arrived early in the morning, had a coffee and waited to be called in. Robert or Dominick would come and collect me from reception. We made small talk. I would change into a surgical gown and walk into the treatment room. The table I laid on only had one leg and it protruded into a round space where patients were given their proton therapy. I called this space my wheel of fortune because the walls revolved around the table I laid on. A massive nozzle which delivers the proton beam is attached to the revolving wall so it can be moved into hundreds of different positions around the patient. Surrounded by these feats of engineering I could have been on the set of a Ridley Scott science fiction movie. My stomach rumbled. Oh no here comes the Alien. False alarm, it's just the constipation.

Once the mask and handcuffs were fitted, I was shuffled around to get me into the right position and X-ray machines would come out of the back wall to help align me with the proton beam. To help me work out where in my neck the massive nozzle would deliver the proton, I visualised myself protruding from the middle of a huge clock face. The room revolved and moved the nozzle slowly to its first position which was below me. On my imaginary clock face it stopped at twenty five minutes past five. Two of my eight brass apertures and a plastic diffuser were fitted into the mouth of the huge nozzle. A loud ping told the radiologists when to leave the room so I could be zapped. The proton beam delivered my radiotherapy into my neck for a minute. It was a bit like listening to a siren somewhere in the distance. The high pitched noise of the siren would build and build until it ran out of steam, when the noise would dissipate slowly like air being let out of a balloon. As the noise deflated Robert and Dominick would return and my wheel of fortune moved the nozzle to the quarter past three position on my imaginary clock face. The next set of brass apertures and a different plastic diffuser were fitted into the nozzle and I was zapped a second time.

I was zapped again twice where the wheel of fortune moved the nozzle to ten past ten and lastly it moved over to my left side where it stopped at quarter to nine. Each day for eleven days I was zapped four times from the same four angles. It took about sixteen minutes during which time I did not move. But why, when this was going on did my nose itch, why did I want to swallow, why did I want to cough, why did I want to scratch my chin or wipe away a tear? All these little things were sent to test my resolve.

One day a guy from FedEx knocked the door of the apartment. He handed John a large cardboard box. Amongst other things it contained wine, teabags, biscuits, my favourite cheese and onion crisps, peanuts, chocolates, two toy guns, colourful sunglasses, a colouring book and pens and a photo of Ballyheigue beach. The box did not include a note or card to say who it was from but from the photograph we knew it must have come from Ireland. But it did include an empty envelope. The card arrived separately several days later. The hamper was from John's nephew Sean and his wife Margaret. The hamper cheered us up no end and we got great pleasure from it. We gave the kiddy things to a family at the hospital over from England.

On one particular day, we had been sitting by the pool for the afternoon when we went back to the flat and John started to get dinner ready. It was a pleasant enough evening, almost benign. We were looking forward to relaxing in front of the television with a movie and then news from home started to come through. Manchester had been hit by a terror attack. A lone bomber had detonated an improvised explosive device in the foyer of a concert hall when an Ariana Grande concert had finished. We found out much later that twenty two people including children died and another one hundred and twenty were injured in the attack. Police told reporters they were treating the incident as a terrorist attack. We both felt sick and somehow guilty we were not home to send our support to the families of those killed or hurt. To not be at home when a tragic national event occurs does make me feel strange. I had experienced the same feelings when I was away on holiday when Lord Mountbatten was murdered in Ireland and when Princess Diana was killed in Paris. It is not good to be remote and feel detached from national tragedies.

One Tuesday we arrived at the hospital to find they were running 15 minutes late. This turned into 100 minutes. We waited until nine thirty before I went in. This happened again when I started my last batch of treatments. I was now to have booster sessions over thirteen days where the nozzle would be moved into a different position every time. The proton beam would be aimed at the pocket where the tumour had sat; or as I visualised it, the foundations of the place where Dolores had squatted all those months. One day I was zapped three times on the right and one on the left. Another day I was zapped twice on the right and twice on the left. Setting me up and getting me in the right position proved to be a bit tricky every time and some days it took longer than was comfortable.

After my treatment sessions we spent a lot of time by the pool. Every day a middle aged man came for a swim in the late afternoon. I always knew when he had arrived. I did not even have to open my eyes because he had a very distinctive way of swimming. He swam the crawl in his own very lazy way. He made a slip, slop, slap drrrrrraaaaag sound as he groaned heavily through the water. I grew accustomed to the deep sounds and it would relax me to the point where I would slowly doze off for a few precious minutes in the late sun.

One Sunday a group of friends had a pool party to celebrate the end of their exams. We had learned from other people living in the complex, that Jacksonville is known as a turnstile city because lots of young people working in insurance, law, medicine or accountancy move to Jacksonville for two or three years and then move on. They come to Jacksonville to enhance or develop their careers by working for prestigious companies, to complete higher degree programmes or gain valuable work experience which is the reason why the average age of the population in Jacksonville is one of the lowest in the US at about 34. Armed with a great résumé young people are able to move to other cities and secure great jobs. I loved the idea of Jacksonville being a turnstile. I now had something in common with these young dynamic people because I had come here on a temporary basis to get my life back and, like them, secure a great future.

The hostess was a beautiful young woman who came over to us to apologise in advance if they got a bit noisy. She told us to let her know if it became too annoying and invited us for a beer and something to eat when the party was in full swing.

'Don't worry about us,' John told her. 'We love parties and the party life. You have fun.'

Her guests of young professionals started arriving in dribs and drabs. They played games, played music and had a great time. One particular guest stood out from the others and I instantly felt sorry for him. He took off his cap in a great flurry to reveal a mop of long hair dyed bright green. He stood by the pool loudly greeting people as he stretched his body. It was not the body of an athlete and I could tell the only machine he used at the gym was the one marked vending. He continued to be loud and he threw balls that hit people who did not want to play. When he left I got a whiff of his pungent exhaust. He made me remember how on occasions when I was young I had not always felt confident. But now I was older I did not think like this anymore. Not everything about getting older is great, but not worrying so much about what people think of you is certainly one of them. Besides, Dolores had taught me to make the most of every minute.

With everything that had happened to me, I would often imagine other things might also be going wrong when they were not. If I got a pain or tickle in a big toe I would worry it might need to be amputated. I had been worrying about my eyes; I thought my eyesight was starting to deteriorate when things were getting a bit blurred. One evening John asked me to read something which popped up on his iPad. I got my glasses and tried to read the message, but I could not see the words clearly. I panicked and told John I was losing my eyesight. I was convinced and I was scared. Then I spotted one of the lenses had fallen out of its frame.

I continued to have my treatments over the next two weeks and then the Jacksonville experience started to run out of steam as it began to draw to a natural end. Up to now we had gone to the hospital every day where we saw the same people we would greet, had got to know and with whom we had exchanged stories.

One of our last outings was with a few friends from the hospital to St Augustine, which is the oldest town in America where we took part in an Art Walk around the town to see the work of visiting artists. It was here in a gallery on the oldest street in America, where I met a retired serviceman with whom I had the scariest conversation. Suddenly and out of nowhere he asked me what I thought of the President.

'Well back home we might say he is a bit like Marmite. Marmite is a very strong spread you can put on toast and people either love it or hate it. He does provoke strong reactions,' I tried not to commit myself one way or the other and be diplomatic. I had learned over the last few months that the office of President is more important than the individual holding the post. I did not want to be rude about the President of a country which I found fascinating and to which I owed so much.

'I love the man,' he said. 'He's going to make us great again.'

'How do you think he will do that?' I asked innocently.

'Well he'll send all the blacks back.' I was shocked by what he said, not just because of his choice of words but because he chose to talk like this to a complete stranger who might not share his political views. I do not think he set out to shock me. I think he just thought it was totally acceptable to express his views no matter what they were and it would not matter to him if I might be offended. He seemed to represent a new kind of cruel confidence.

'Where will he send them?' I asked.

'Back home, to where they fucking belong.'

'But this is their home. They have been here for over two hundred years haven't they?' I asked. He shrugged his shoulders.

'You'll see,' he said as he ended the conversation with a chilling wink. I shuddered. I was glad he walked away to re-join a couple of friends.

Then as if to hammer home how vile and cruel the world can be, a news story popped up on my iPad when we got back to the apartment. I rushed to put on the television to be told a van had been deliberately driven into pedestrians on London Bridge before crashing on the south bank of the River Thames. The three terrorists then ran into nearby Borough Market where they stabbed people in restaurants and pubs. These murderers killed eight people and injured another forty eight in my home town on the streets where only six years ago I had an office. But they were shot dead by police. It was strange to think how the hatred of the man I met in the art gallery and the terrorists compared so badly with the kindness and care I had experienced over the last year.

We had attended regular surgeries with Dr Rotondo and

Michelle and we were doing all the routine stuff of life like shopping, cleaning and doing the washing and then we got the phone call to tell us our return flights to London had been booked. Our temporary life was nearly over. This news confirmed to me how quickly the time had gone since I painted the house in Ballyheigue back in 2015. Time had flown by because I had been forced to manage my reactions to the cancer and cope with all that happened. Cancer had changed my relationship with time; blocks of time had been swallowed up managing twelve months of increasing pain, sorting out the diagnosis and getting through those operations, periods of recovery and radiotherapy.

The final day of treatment arrived. We went to the hospital as normal but we saw fewer people we knew. The reception area was full of new faces. The group of guys who had been there every day and to whom we wished good morning was gone. The ladies who had enjoyed each other's chatter every day were no longer there. Even a few of our close friends had disappeared back to their homes across the States.

I went for my last treatment. I had an exit interview with the head of admissions. I had a final meeting with Dr Rotondo and Michelle. I was given a detailed report of my treatment. We went upstairs to the Wednesday lunch where I told the story about the nurse in England who told the older gentleman in the bed next to me the drugs he was being given did not work on people over the age of sixty. The story got a good laugh.

'Being told you have cancer is awful. It's so tough and it will change your life,' I told my audience. 'But it comes with lots of good and bad experiences. It's true, being in pain is horrible and having horrendous and intrusive surgery and coping with periods of challenging recovery is scary. I was of course zapped no end of times downstairs. But has it been worth it? Would I do it again? Yes of course I would. I know it is strange, but I am weirdly grateful for the experience. My strength of character has been tested and I have discovered new things about myself; my strength of resolve and my weaknesses.

'I have been treated and looked after by the best in the world who said they would give me my life back. You will definitely meet people here who can make you better, if you let them. Work with these wonderful people and do as you are told. I have enjoyed the love and support of family, friends, old work colleagues, neighbours and even some strangers I met on the way. I have not enjoyed having cancer, that of course would be silly, but I have enjoyed all the experiences I've had. Funny things will happen, so use the funny bits to stay positive. Thank you.' The audience clapped loudly and cheers broke out.

We went downstairs to the reception where I had photos taken with Dr Rotondo, Michelle and Gerry. I ran the 'Aud Chime', which everybody rings on the last day of their treatment to tell everyone they had finished. The chime hangs in the reception of the centre and was given by the family of an Australian lady called Audrey. On the last chime, my stomach felt strangely empty and the ache in my now weightless body made me feel hopelessly sad at the thought of leaving the centre for the last time. My head swam and in the confusion I was vaguely aware of people thanking me for what I said at the lunch and as I kissed cheeks and shook hands I was saying good bye to my heroes. The time to return to London now seemed right. It was time to take our leave. Our time in Jacksonville had run its course and we had become has-beens.

It was one of those wonderful moments when an aeroplane seems to hover for a few seconds after take-off as it turns into its flightpath so it can then zoom to where it needs to go. I looked down on the huge expanse of Miami and watched the sun sparkle on the waves through a light summer mist that softened the mass of buildings and roads. As Miami faded we started our return to London, where Mrs May was being confirmed as Prime Minister after her near election disaster and I thought about the future. Was Dolores under control? Had Dolores left the building? Was my dance with Dolores over? I would not know for another three months how successful the radiotherapy had been. Time would tell. I touched the back of John's hand and my smile told him thank you.

Epilogue

I still have cancer. On December 22nd 2017 I was told Dolores had gone. The operations and proton beam treatment were 100% successful. My spine and nervous system are now safe. Unfortunately, a few rogue cells escaped during one of my operations and embedded themselves in soft tissue. They are not thought to be life threatening and are not near any major organs. I should be okay and it should be possible to manage these cancer cells using a variety of techniques. I had radiotherapy for 25 days over five weeks in early 2018. I had cryotherapy in November 2018 and March 2019, which is a procedure used to freeze tumours.

How many adventures can one person have in one lifetime?

Timeline of Events

Month	Year	Event
June	2015	Holiday in Ireland I first felt a pain in my neck, which I thought was caused by the effort of painting the outside of the house.
August	2015	First visit to my GP Pain killers were prescribed for the pain in my neck.
October	2015	Holiday in Ireland We stayed in a hotel in Kenmare, the pain was awful and it ruined one particular dinner for me.
November	2015	Second visit to my GP I was referred to a physiotherapist.
December	2015	Rushed to emergency in an ambulance I thought my neck had broken. The doctor told me to buy a new pillow and gave me painkillers.
December	2015	First visit to physiotherapist Could it be rheumatism?

January	2016	Second visit to physiotherapist I was given stretching exercises using a towel.
February	2016	Third visit to physiotherapist The physiotherapist said I should be referred to a hospital for further investigation, but I was told an appointment would not be guaranteed.
March	2016	Holiday in Cape Verde This was one of the last times I remember feeling well.
April	2016	Chased the appointments booking number They had my request but were not going to act on it because of shrinking funds. But an officer rang me back with an appointment for July.
May	2016	Holiday on train in Scotland The pain was getting worse and I was finding it difficult to walk.
June	2016	Holiday in Ireland The pain was getting really serious now and it was affecting everything. My neck swelled.
July	2016	Visit to Chelsea and Westminster Hospital Tests were done over four days and

		the tumour was identified.
July	2016	Visit to Charing Cross Hospital Cancer is confirmed and the biopsy left me in even more pain.
July	2016	Charing Cross Hospital confirmed they could not help I was referred to the National Hospital for Neurology and Neurological Surgery.
August	2016	Two visits to the National Hospital I had two meetings with Dr Russo.
September	2016	Consultation with Mr Choi Mr Choi told me what would happen.
September	2016	First major operation Surgery lasted nine hours and I lost three litres of blood. Tumour attacked through the back of my neck.
October	2016	Second major operation Surgery was carried out by a team of twenty two people and again lasted over nine hours. Tumour attacked through my jaw and the front of my neck.
November	2016	Convalescence at home

December	2016	Celebrated Christmas Managed to go to parties and spent Christmas with family.
January	2017	First visit to Florida
January	2017	Tumour returns I returned to London for more surgery.
February	2017	Blood clot and third major operation I had to recover from a bold clot on my left lung. Tumour attacked through the side of my neck.
March	2017	Returned to Florida
April	2017	Radiotherapy using photon beam therapy
May	2017	Radiotherapy using proton beam therapy
June	2017	Last proton beam treatment
Onwards		The first day of the rest of my life

The things people say

Since we have been home from Florida a few things have been said that raised a smile.

1. We were driving back from Ireland in June 2017, when we stopped for lunch in Lismore. Lismore is a real beauty spot with its cathedral and castle and we particularly like the cafes and tea shops. We had had lunch in one of its cafes when an elderly lady came in for her coffee. Having noticed I was holding up my head with my left hand under my chin, she asked me if I had toothache. I told her no and explained I had a rare bone cancer.

   'Oh you poor thing,' she said sympathetically. 'Pat over the road in the pub had cancer. We buried him yesterday.'

   We bid her farewell and left laughing.

2. Later the same day we were in Rosslare. It was a lovely evening and so we went for a walk on the beach. Again I was holding my chin. As we left the beach three very smart middle aged ladies were sitting on a park bench. One asked if I had a headache. I explained my predicament and said walking was made easier when I hold my head up. One of the ladies jumped up, held her chin and tucked her other hand between the top her legs.

   'Good job you didn't get the cancer down here as well,' she shouted. 'You'd have to hobble around like this,' she said as she jumped around in a circle to demonstrate what she meant. 'Never mind your both gorgeous,' she finished.

We walked back to the car laughing.

3. We met a couple of friends in the hospital in March 2018. We were talking about our problems and one of the friends asked me if my cancer was in the neck. I told him it was.

    'My mother had cancer in the neck. She was dead in three months,' he said. He is mid European; perhaps the treatment is not so good where he comes from.

4. We were in a restaurant one evening and the waitress asked about my neck and we talked about my operations. A little later she asked John if I was Phillip Schofield because of my white hair. He said no and I told her I was George Clooney. She told me I would need a lot more operations to look like Gorgeous George; a lot more.

5. My turn:

    When I meet people I have not seen for ages they often ask me what it is like to have rods in my neck. I tell them it is okay and I tell them about the bolts in my skull. One sticks out a bit as a bump. 'Do you want to touch my knob?' I always ask.

About the author

Before cancer James enjoyed good health. Before taking early retirement he worked in education and was awarded the MBE for services to Apprenticeships. His experiences have taught him to be positive about life's challenges.

This is his first book.